TRUTH & FREEDOM

A Match Made In Heaven

Antivirus Protection for Your Cranial Computer

TRUTH & FREEDOM

A Match Made In Heaven

Antivirus Protection for Your Cranial Computer

Les Huntley

Copyright **2013**, All Rights Reserved

Intermountain North Publishing

CONTENTS

INTRODUCTION 1

CHPATER I. 5
What, Why and How

CHAPTER II. 15
The Firewall

CHAPTER III. 49
The Truthalizer

CHAPTER IV, 67
The TruthApp in Action

CHAPTER V. 101
The LieBot in Action

CHAPTER VI. 125
Applications

CHAPTER VII. 133
The Resuscitated Church

APPENDIX I. 145
Introduction to "The Ten Commandments of Propaganda"

APPENDIX II. 167
Fifty-two Named Propaganda Techniques

APPENDIX III. 177
The Record of Chapter IV.

Dedicated to:

My sons, the two I love more than any other men;

Guy Myrick Huntley, my firstborn son
Named for his grandfather and great-great-great grandfather
Courageous and honorable men both

Jason Leslie Huntley, my lastborn son,
Named for his father and a distant Scottish ancestor

May both be richly blessed all the days of their lives!

Acknowledgements

This book could not have been written without the knowing or unknowing assistance of many others. I wish to acknowledge here several of those who have had a great impact on the work. They are:

Donna Mae Huntley, the wife who for 53 years has supported and encouraged me in anything I tried to do, even when she didn't fully understand what that was and why I was doing it. Her shared wisdom often keeps me from making blunders, especially those that might puzzle or offend my readers.

Dr. Brian Anse Patrick, whose book, Ten *Commandments of Propaganda,* gave me needed insights into the workings of that nefarious art, and who has kindly permitted me to use portions of his book in this one.

Mr. Hendikus (Henk) Lit, my mentor and friend whose life and example continue to inspire me to attempt the impossible and to be fearless in doing what I am called to do.

Pastor Bill Gunter, a friend, a mentor in things spiritual, and an example of what it means to be a man who walks with Christ.

Pastor John Stroupe, another friend and mentor, who consistently sharpens me in the same way iron sharpens iron and one man sharpens another.

Francis L. (Frank) Huntley, my brother, an ex Marine and living proof there is no such thing, whose brilliant mind, utter honesty and sometime bluntness in speaking truth have inspired me to always try harder to be better and stronger.

Les Huntley

June, 2013

A Match Made In Heaven
INTRODUCTION

Wisdom is the comprehension of what is true coupled with optimum judgment as to action. (Wikipedia)

This is a book about wisdom, about how to obtain it so you can make choices that benefit **you** in the present and the future.

Having wisdom, knowing what is really true and knowing how to apply that knowledge is the key to living a free life. Jesus said nearly **2000** years ago, *"If you are truly my disciples, you shall know the truth, and the truth shall set you free."* So you see truth and freedom go together just like a man and woman bound together by a match made in heaven.

This is not a finished work, it has been under construction for over ten years, and would require at least another ten for me to complete it. But I am a very senior citizen, my remaining days are limited, and I must trust those who take to heart what they read here to write the next one, two or ten volumes in my stead.

As for me, the book tends to grow as I learn each new bit of truth. Just this morning while contemplating how to present the material in a way that will support its new title, I realized I will have to rewrite this Introduction and maybe the following chapters as well. With me, rewriting a chapter too often means expanding it, so the book always grows. Enough is enough! It is time to write FINISH and send it to the publisher!

The subtitle promises "antivirus protection for your cranial computer" and that is one of the goals here. Before continuing, I must pause to say what I say next is not intended to be a rigorous description of how the brain functions and wisdom is acquired. It is but an analogous description that helps me lead you readers into the discussion from my point of view. Read on and you will see what I mean.

Each of us entered the world equipped with a wondrous on-board biological computer complete with fleshly hardware and

Truth & Freedom

with firmware that equips it with the ability to add random access memory (RAM) limited only by the span of its body's competent life. The program embedded in the firmware controls essential functions, commanding its body to pump blood, breathe, drink, eat, grow, protect itself from harm, seek pleasurable experiences, avoid unpleasant ones, and above all avoid damage and death.

In the beginning, and perhaps extending throughout life, all actions are initiated by the firmware; we call these early automatic actions instinctive. Then, as the body grows and sensory abilities are perfected, the computer begins to experience the world outside the body. It quickly learns that certain behaviors are followed by feeding, cuddling, soothing sounds and other pleasant experiences. It quickly learns as well that some behaviors evoke unpleasant responses from its environment; throwing its body on the floor and causing it to kick and scream being one of them.

These experiences are stored in RAM, where they are accessed when the firmware perceives action is needed. As time passes and the body and abilities grow, more and more of these experiences are stored in RAM, and now influence nearly all the body's actions. If the environment is a "good" one this amounts to beneficial programming which leads to a healthy pleasant life for the body and its computer. If the environment is otherwise the opposite is true.

As the body grows and acquires the ability to speak and understand what others are saying,–these abilities are stored in RAM of course–personal experience begins to be supplemented by the experiences of others communicated verbally. At first many of these are tested, for example by touching a hot object to see if what Mommy says is true. After a sufficient number of such experiments, the computer decides Mommy is a reliable source of truth, and what she says is automatically stored in RAM.

A Match Made In Heaven

As time progresses, the number of "reliable sources" grows with experience. By the time the child enters school, he/she has been told to listen to and obey the teacher. This information is stored in RAM as having come from Mommy and Daddy and other reliable sources. Here is where the child enters the danger zone.

The result of this transfer of authority was not a problem in America as few as **60** years ago when parents carefully monitored what their children were being taught and made sure their teachers were upright citizens and reliable coaches for their progeny. Today none of that is true. Parents, being a product of the public schools have themselves been programmed into entrusting their children to teachers and schools to be formed into the useful well adjusted citizens they want them to be.

The problem comes from the fact that self seeking men discovered many, many years ago they could control others' actions by controlling what they believe is true. By programming them, the programmers are able to assure the programmed will act in ways that benefit the programmer, often with the ones so programmed experiencing results harmful to their own interests. That malicious programming is what I mean by a cranial computer virus. "Virus" may not convey exactly the right image to your mind, so I have used the word "malware" elsewhere instead.

Carrying the analogy a little further, this book is intended to do several things: First, **to alert you to the fact** that your on-board computer is under attack and that you must defend yourself. Second, to provide you a *Firewall* to protect your most-personal-computer from being infected by malware(*Chapter II.*). Third, to introduce you to a process for extracting true statements from a collection of information I'll call that our *Truthalyzer–(Chapter III.)*. And finally to show you what your world might be like if applying what you find herein leads you to the same understanding of truth that I have found.

Truth & Freedom

The ***Truthalyzer*** has three applications, for two of which I give detailed examples showing how to use them. The first is extracting reliably true, i.e. credible, statements from a mass of information. I'll call that our ***TruthApp*** (Example in Chapter IV.). The second is testing conclusions presented to us as true to see if they are reliability supported by evidence. I call that our ***LieBot*** (Example in chapter V.) The third I might call our ***Whichifier***, but won't; too much is too much after all! It is a procedure for deciding between two credible and mutually exclusive alternatives, and is briefly discussed in Chapter III., but not by **that** name.

Many who read what I've written above will immediately reject it, not realizing they have been carefully programmed to have just that reaction to anything that might lead them to question the source of their ideas and attitudes. "*You may imagine yourself unaffected by propaganda, but the person who thinks himself above propaganda is quite possibly its creature.*" is a true statement. Understanding it and accepting its truth is essential to throwing off enslaving chains and regaining lost freedom.

A Match Made In Heaven
CHAPTER I.

What, Why and How

Americans live their lives blissfully unaware of the ideological chains binding them, imagining they still have the freedoms guaranteed by their 225 year old Constitution. That they might have been tricked by a hundred years long propaganda campaign into voluntarily surrendering those freedoms never enters their minds.

Propaganda is a highly structured and well funded industry established to control a population by altering and controlling its beliefs about themselves and their world. It uses many attack modes to alter the population's conception of reality, with the intent always of deceiving in one way or another; and that deception always aims to further the interests of propagandists at the expense of its targets.

For the younger among you, it will help to think of propagandists as hackers who inject malware into your most personal, personal computers, your brains. No dirty trick is off limits to propagandists but most attacks use the equivalent of **worms** and **spyware**. The worms are designed to mess with your mental software to the extent that you no longer act to benefit yourself, but choose acts that benefit your controllers.

You think you choose freely, but can in fact too often make the choice you were preprogrammed to make. Pavlov rang his bell and his dogs salivated. There is no difference for anyone thoroughly propagandized, and that describes a large majority of Americans today.

Propagandists use their **spyware** to accomplish two goals, first, to discover the population's interests, desires, fears, etc. so they can design their **worms** to obtain desired actions and second to monitor their propaganda's effect in order to improve its impact. Their worms are the lies, distortions, distractions, diversions; anything and everything they can generate to keep you from knowing truth and get you to believe what they want you to believe.

It is essential to know truth and it is equally important to know that you are being propagandized, for until you know that, you won't know you need to begin searching for truth. Truth is the bolt cutter that lops off the chains of slavery, freeing men and women to be what they were designed to be.

Seventy years ago, independent, competing elements of the press and academia still existed and information came to the masses primarily as words printed on paper. Today that independence and competition are gone from both the press and academia; both are now tightly controlled by propagandists pushing one cause or another.

Very little actual information is stored in printed form today, and much previously so stored has been converted to digital form where it can be altered to hide the truth forever and used to feed the controlled falsified information. Thankfully, much of the history important to today's men and women is recorded in books and papers which cannot be altered without detection, but be on the lookout for the future equivalent of mass book burnings. Truth is poison to propaganda, and propagandists will do anything to keep their targets from finding it.

Truth frees, lies enslave. Uncounted billions of atheists, Jews, Buddhists, Hindus, communists, Darwinists, pagans, two billion Christians and one billion Muslims all live lesser lives than they could be living. What do they have in common? All are slaves to unknown masters. *How can that be*, you ask; *I'm not a slave to anyone, nor was my father, or his father before him. How can you say I am a slave?*

Let me put it this way, you aren't really a slave because you are not the property of anyone but yourself, but you and every one of those mentioned above live like slaves, live a lesser life than all would live if they were living in the freedom they really have. All are living as slaves because they believe lies, untruths. Believing any lie, any untruth, makes it impossible for you to

A Match Made In Heaven

choose the better way, the way you would choose if you knew the truth.

Don't take my word for it; let me briefly introduce you here to the ***Ten Commandments of Propaganda***, authored by Dr. Brian Anse Patrick.

Introduction

You have already been worked in a subtle way. How? Although the title of this book is The Ten Commandments of Propaganda, you will actually find eleven commandments here, and much other information beside. The reference to the Ten Commandments accesses something already stored in your brain, waiting. The title calls and activates it with virtually no effort on your part. In an instant you already understand pretty much the whole drift of a fairly complicated concept that I am proposing. You know that you have encountered a set of precepts, shalts and shalt-nots, designed to guide thought and behavior. And by merely understanding all this, you are now well on the way to being persuaded of what I will have to say, for to understand is perhaps half way to being persuaded.

My task would be much more difficult if I had to assemble this whole idea from basic elements. Simply put, for any propaganda to be effective as mass persuasion, it must somehow resonate with ideas that are already in people's heads. To do otherwise is to attempt an entirely new installation of ideas and concepts, which requires far too much work on your part. So I have done the work for you, a sort of cognitive pre-packaging that takes advantage of the human propensity for efficiently avoiding work.

But don't mistake propaganda for a mere set of tricks. Nor am I trying to propagandize you at the moment, just trying to demonstrate a technique that I hope will draw your interest. I am acting within my role as a professor who has been intensely interested in propaganda for many years. And while professors (and writers) have quite often been propagandists for various causes, good and evil, wittingly and unwittingly, what I attempt here is merely to share a set of principles codified in the course of teaching and research. I do here what professors are supposed to do in an ideal world, which is to profess what they believe to be true and useful based on judgment, experience ... and familiarity with a wide and deep body of well-vetted work that has been produced on their topic of specialization.

One might say this is education—beware, though, because education has, as often as not, conveyed a great deal of propaganda, and highly educated people tend to be more, not less, susceptible to propaganda than are the uneducated. However, I prefer to think of my effort here as a continuation of a conversation that has been ongoing for many years in western culture. You may at some point wish to participate in this conversation.

Also, more pragmatically, you may quite likely find this book useful for both offense and defense in your personal and professional life. You may imagine yourself unaffected by propaganda, but the person who thinks himself above propaganda is quite possibly its creature.

*So here is my method. Although propaganda is an immense modern undertaking, I have tried to keep the text sparse and readable. After this introduction, in which I will attempt a synopsis of propaganda's arrival on the modern scene, I will move right on to the Commandments. ... The purpose here is to promote readability without sacrificing depth or technical correctness. ... Any preaching on my part will be also confined to endnotes (*removed in this excerpt*). The*

A Match Made In Heaven

endnotes also summarize and comment on significant books, research papers, and their authors, including a few classic propaganda films (which I encourage you to watch online so as to better understand these "timeless" principles.)

The endnotes themselves provide a fairly good overview of history, research, and techniques of propaganda— especially within propaganda's social-scientific sister disciplines; for a great deal of social science, theory and method, especially social psychology, has been linked quite directly with improving or discovering mechanisms of propaganda. For example, survey research, now a universal practice, was essentially brought into widespread service in order to measure susceptibilities and effects of propaganda on target populations.

Each Commandment has its own chapter, although each can be applied in many ways, as befits general principles. The Commandments are simple, but have ramifying applications that will be suggested via straightforward examples. This may sometimes lead to a bit of overlap between the Commandments in their applications, but (while) each Commandment has an action-principle, its action-principle remains nonetheless distinct. I will often employ extreme examples because they more clearly illustrate principles.

Just as it is in nowise the first, this book cannot in any sense be the last word on propaganda. This field of endeavor is too big, too specialized, too pressing, too ongoing for such a book to even exist.

Propaganda has become one of the grand undertakings of modernity. Without it there could be no bureaucratic-corporate organizations or states, mass democratic or otherwise, for just as humans are characterized by an ability to communicate with each other, modern

Truth & Freedom

bureaucratic administrative organizations are characterized by a reliance on propaganda, both externally and internally.

Propaganda is a chief means by which the organizations that dominate modern life try to communicate power.

That last sentence contains one bit of information the truth seeker absolutely must have; we are controlled by organizations using propaganda not just to control us but to make sure we stay controlled. I won't include Dr. Patrick's complete Introduction here because that would too greatly interrupt the narrative. Please be sure to read it (**Appendix I**) either now or after you finish what I have written. It's just too important to miss.

You want examples of control? Try this. Two hundred thirty-some years ago, our forefathers brought forth on the North American continent a new nation, conceived in liberty and dedicated to the proposition that all men are created equal. (Thank you, Abe Lincoln!) Did you get that? *In liberty*; **free**, **sovereign** men established a new nation. **Created equal**; no man being any better, having any more rights, any more value or any higher authority than any other man. All sovereign, all equal in their sovereignty, governing themselves by laws and rules established by mutual consent to promote the common good.

Is that the United States we see today? It absolutely is not! (You should have answered *Well, DUH!* to that question.) We are ruled, in a most kingly fashion, by *Elites*, as their minions endlessly describe them. These elites – our ruling class – have piled up for themselves many rights on top of those the fathers recognized, rights the fathers could never have guessed a free people **could** let men claim for themselves. Our laws are ignored, our treasury is looted to enrich the ruling class; our rulers use **our** money to buy anything and everything they

A Match Made In Heaven

imagine will maintain **them** in positions of luxury, power and prestige.

I could go on and on, talking about lost property rights, children forcefully taken from parents, industries destroyed by sending factories overseas, escalating prices caused by excessive borrowing, etc., etc., etc. But I won't. Let's talk instead about how we got ourselves into this mess.

We are in this mess simply because we did not act as sovereign men and women, and we did that because we didn't know we were **responsible** for acting as sovereigns. We delegated our responsibility, often without the slightest idea we were doing so, to men who lied, promising us anything that would induce us to surrender our authority to them bit by bit.

Truth matters! If we don't know the truth we cannot be free; believing lies has made us slaves. We don't know the truth because our parents delegated to the educational system their responsibility for teaching us truth. And the educators didn't and don't teach us how to find truth for ourselves; they have all unknowingly become propagandists for those who enslave us. It wasn't entirely our parents' fault we don't know truth – their parents didn't teach them enough truth either so our parents had precious little truth to pass along to us.

Even worse off than we are our children who we have entrusted, not to the smaller schools of our youth, but to the Department of Education, an agency that has become part of the largest, most effective propaganda agency anywhere. The establishment keeps us in ideological slavery by a constant flood of editorials, slanted newscasts, deliberate lies and shameless propaganda. If we are to live free we must learn to protect ourselves, to cut through the lies, omissions and propaganda and find the truth.

Truth matters; we must know truth if we are to choose wisely, choose actions that really will be best for us in the long run.

Truth & Freedom

And because so much of what we believe, what we "know is true," is communicated to us by others, we must learn how to know **who** we can trust to tell us the truth.

Truth Seekers, please do not abandon this work when you find that I am using the Christian Bible to illustrate techniques. There is a reason for using that source that has nothing to do with anyone's belief system; I use it here as a teaching tool. It is a complete, closed data set that won't be changed by later discoveries. In using it, we can be sure any conclusions we reach about what it teaches can never be overturned by newly found information. That is important because by using it we avoid distracting discussions wondering if information not yet discovered will come along to negate the truths we find.

My hope for this increasingly not so little book is that in reading it you will learn three things – **how to know who to trust to tell you the truth, how to dig the truth out of a mass of information, including propaganda,** and **how to test the truth of what others communicate to you.**

Now I hope I haven't misled you into thinking only the good old U-S-of-A is messed up; everything is messed up all over the world. Consider religion, for example. Muslims are enslaved by a book designed to control, not to free. Hindus are enslaved by the caste system, Buddhists by a philosophy and Darwinists by a flawed science based on false assumptions.

Do not think Christianity has escaped. For one thousand years Christ's Church lived in unity, believing what its leaders found written in God's Book, the Bible. Then error crept in, a seed was planted, unity destroyed. Rome, believing a lie, left its sister bishoprics, splitting what was until then an unblemished union,

That first lie led to another, then two more, then a flood of lies. Today Christendom struggles for existence in tens of thousands of competing fiefdoms, each fighting to keep its

A Match Made In Heaven

captives from being stolen by competitors, forgotten unity a faded dream.

For 500 years after that first lie was believed by the Church, dedicated, honest, able men struggled to find the truths written in God's Book. They did not find truth; they could not, for they were using the wrong tools, the tools of philosophy and theology, basing their search on unchallenged and false assumptions. **They needed tools not yet invented**, the tools of the technician, the troubleshooter, the scientist.

A technician goes to the manufacturer's instruction manual to learn how a malfunctioning instrument was designed to work and what devices inside the instrument make it work that way. He systematically tests each device to see if it is doing what it was intended to do. A master technician lacking the means for testing a device constructs his own tester. Then he publishes what he has learned as a help to others who encounter the same malfunctioning device.

This book is that kind of report, written by one with over 40 years experience in troubleshooting not only instruments but also concepts, procedures, theories, building his own testers, then reporting his findings in peer reviewed journals and Conference Proceedings. Here I will show you how to do that kind of work yourself, how to decide who to believe, how to find for yourself what to believe, and how to test the validity of others' positions on matters important to you.

As we get into this (I say we because we will be doing this together.) you will find that one of the hardest parts of finding truth is deciding what data sources to use in your search. Much of what is written, spoken, presented in media is deliberately designed to keep us from knowing truth, so it can be a daunting task to determine what we should believe and what we should not. We will discuss tools for identifying propaganda; using those tools will help us find the truth propagandists want to hide from us.

Truth & Freedom

As I said above, we will use the Christian scriptures, the Old and New Testaments, as the data source for the examples we will work through in the following. In this study, we will assume the Bible contains God's message to mankind, and we will assume every word (in the ancient language) was put there on purpose to teach somebody, somewhere, sometime, something that is important for him/her to know. For this present project, we will simply assume those things, and not worry about deciding if they are true. **Assumptions like this one must be tested and confirmed before we base our lives on them, but that goes far beyond what we'll be doing here.**

Please, if you are one of the many truth seekers who question, even deny, the validity of the Bible, don't let that discourage you from completing this study. I want to teach you to use tools that will help you decide **who** you should believe and **what** you should believe. I want to do that for selfish purposes – setting you free will help me in my struggle to be free. Because the Bible is what it is, it is an excellent source for teaching those principles.

I leave this brief introduction with two final thoughts: Famous (infamous to some of you) atheist. Richard Dawkins, in his book *The God Delusion* quotes another atheist's 11th Commandment – **Question Everything**.

That is advice well taken. Ignore the source if you must, but use it to get free and stay free; apply it to every communication that tries to tell you what to do – including this one which is not meant to mislead but may inadvertently do so. And remember always: **Propagandists are not your friends;** consider them at best antagonists in a one-sided contest designed to separate you from something you value

A Match Made In Heaven
CHAPTER II.

The Firewall

Who Should I Believe

In August, 1945, I was 16 years old and living in rural poverty in Idaho's backwoods. On a dark, rainy day, I learned from my Uncle Pat's radio that the war with Japan was over, that the Japanese had unconditionally surrendered. I remember slogging the muddy half mile home through the woods and fields, cold, wet, more than half angry and bitterly disappointed. I had been living for the day I would turn 17 and could join the Marines and go kill Japs.

How did a good, peace loving, country boy come to such an outlandish ambition? It was simply that I had fallen under the spell of a persistent propaganda campaign specifically designed to accomplish just that with every American male.

I had listened to stories of the sneak attack on Pearl Harbor, the courageous but futile resistance of American troops on Wake Island, the battle of Bataan, the fall of Corregidor and the Bataan Death March. I had heard President Roosevelt's Fireside Chats, absorbing every bit of propaganda designed to increase the patriotic fervor of the American populace.

And, yes, I had seen the Life Magazine photos of dead Marines washing up on the beaches of Tarawa, but to one who had never experienced the death of a close friend or family member, one to whom hardship and privation were a part of life, none of that really mattered. I hated Japs, and firmly believed the only good Jap was a dead Jap. And, yes, I knew about napalm, and white phosphorus, and fire bombing cities full of civilians, but, hey, that's war, and those are very good ways to kill people who would love to kill you first.

Truth & Freedom

It wasn't a perfect propaganda campaign; surely the British, Germans and Japanese had better success than the American machine did. But it was good enough to get millions of men and women to make sacrifices they would never otherwise have made, and it made the difference in deciding the war.

Those of us who lived through that time remember the ration books, the shortage of fuel, tires, cars, food and medicine, the military draft, the Blue Star and Gold Star Mothers, and yes, we remember too the many who suffered none of those hardships because they had friends in high places and money to purchase the favor of those responsible for running the programs supporting those things.

It's certain that WWII would have had a much different outcome had the American elites not waged that war against the generally pacifist and largely isolationist American populace. That fact would seem to be sufficient to justify waging the propaganda war. But is that, in fact, true? What if those who waged the propaganda wars were the ones who caused the war in the first place?

Probably that will never be known. The victors write the history books, and anything that conflicts with the official story – the narrative – quickly disappears from view. But you can be sure that the population of every country engaged in the struggle was firmly convinced **their country was in the right**, and they were doing only what they needed to do to survive.

Whether the world's populations might have been able to ward off the coming conflagration will never be known. But it is clear that without the systematic coloring and distorting of truth, that war could never have reached the violence and destruction it did. One pernicious after effect of that war was the emergence of **a perfected means for controlling a population's actions by controlling its beliefs**.

A Match Made In Heaven

One application of that control is seen in the persistent merchandising that we are subjected to each hour of each day via internet, newspapers, magazines, social media and television – the media generally. Another, fresh in my mind as I write this in April 2013, was the billion dollar propaganda battle waged to determine whether our "first black president" would serve a second term. A third is the media campaign even today being waged to keep the American citizenry from learning whether that person is even eligible to serve as President, or if his name really is Barack Obama.

All such campaigns have one thing in common; their success depends on keeping their targets from knowing the truth. Automobile advertisements tout features their model has that competing models do not, the advantages of its financing plan over others, the social status that comes from owning that model, etc. Never mentioned is a poor frequency of repair record, high cost of ownership, anything that might queer the sale.

Many millions of dollars were spent in the Florida 2012 GOP primary by one candidate to convince the voters that his opponent had no chance to defeat the incumbent, all the while carefully avoiding any mention of his own failure to exceed 25% support in any previous campaign. His opponent largely ignored the attacks of the other, while hammering on that one's many glaring weaknesses. The intent seemed to be to so dominate the discussion by irrelevant information that the truth would never be known.

On January 26th, 2012, the person calling himself Barack H. Obama and his attorney failed to appear at a civil trial called to determine whether he was constitutionally eligible to serve as president of the United States. Evidence and legal precedents were put in the record supporting plaintiffs' allegations that he was not qualified and thus should be barred from appearing on the Georgia primary ballot. By failing to appear and provide evidence and/or legal precedents contrary to those allegations, he essentially conceded the point that he was not eligible.

Media coverage of those events was telling. All but a very few print and television media ignored the trial. Those that did address it used their coverage to discourage its readers/viewers from checking to see it there was any basis for the allegations. This is an excellent example of Dr. Patrick's first commandment of propaganda, ***Control the flow of information.***

MSNBC in one notable many minute long diatribe resorted to name calling, patently false or misleading statements and ridicule of the idea and of any person stupid enough to believe for a second there may be something to the allegations. Here could be a textbook example of the abuse of logic in argument.

I've taken a lot of your time (and perhaps your patience) describing events that have had or might now have very little impact on your personal life, your personal challenges. If you'll stick with me for a few more pages, you will see that it is vitally important for you to know the truth when faced with these far reaching, potentially life changing and surely freedom threatening efforts to control what you believe. With your permission (you can close the book or skip ahead at any time, hence the request for permission) I will share another story illustrating a more immediate, personal need for knowing who to believe.

In the summer of **1952**, I was discharged from the US Navy with about **$1,000** I had saved from my pay over the previous four years. I needed transportation, which in rural Idaho meant wheels. I knew nothing about buying cars so I asked my Dad to help me choose one and keep me from wasting my money on a clunker.

After shopping the local markets for a few hours, I spotted a nice looking '47 Nash sedan at a prosperous looking dealership owned by a man Dad knew had a good reputation in the

A Match Made In Heaven

community. That it was a Nash raised an alarm; Dad had never heard anything good about Nash. But the car looked good, the tires had good tread, the engine compartment and radiator were clean; everything looked really good.

Dad, a Chevy man and untrusting of all things Nash, raised the issue of reliability. The dealer pulled out pages of records showing all the work that had been done on the car. Those records showed the engine had been completely overhauled prior to the car being put on the lot, and that clinched the deal for Dad. So I plunked down $750 of my $1,000, checked and saw the gas tank was half full, and drove the car home.

The bloom was soon off the rose, to use the old cliché, when a few days later I took it to a neighboring town to show it off to a couple of buddies. I ended up taking them for a ride down Lawyer's Canyon a few miles from town only to have the engine quit, leaving us stranded. We checked everything, battery good (engine cranked), good spark, gas gauge showing half full. Nothing!

Then someone had the bright idea of poking a stick down the gas filler tube to see if the tank really was half full. (Yes, in the days before anti-siphon devices, you could do that. Everyone I knew carried a little hose to get a bit of gas to help him down the road to a station.) Bad news; the tank was empty. A little investigation (climbing under and looking up) showed the tank had been dented by a rock or something, so the gauge read half full when the tank was empty.

Eventually some of our friends came looking for us, gave us a little gas via that faithful hose, and we returned home. The bloom was off the rose, but the real faith buster came a few months later when I heard the clatter, clatter, clatter that meant I'd lost a rod bearing. I got someone to tow me to my Uncle Jack's place where he had an empty shed I could use as a garage while I repaired the engine.

Truth & Freedom

Up till then, I was only disgusted. Bad luck! But when I dropped the pan and pulled the piston I completely lost my cool. The piston was shot, and the rings were badly worn. Investigation showed all the rod bearings, the main bearings and all the rings were completely worn out. The engine obviously hadn't been overhauled; the dealer had faked the repair records. But how could the engine be in such bad shape after being driven only the miles showing on the odometer? Oh! Stupid question! If a man will lie about an overhaul, he won't hesitate to roll back an odometer.

Believing those lies because I trusted the integrity of the one telling them cost me 75% of the money I'd worked hard to save over the past four years. It cost me a couple of years of hard work and scraping by to make up for trusting someone not worth trusting.

Realize it or not, you are faced constantly with that kind of scheme to separate you from your money, your freedom, maybe even your life. I can't show you how to be sure you won't fall prey to those schemes, but I can show you a few tools you can use to tip the odds in your favor. That is my task for this chapter, so here goes:

You are, all of us are, constantly bombarded with messages from family, friends and strangers. Most aren't worth wasting time wondering if we should believe them. Mostly these messages are meant for fun, relationship building or getting necessary work done, not for getting us to do something we wouldn't ordinarily do. In a good family and among true friends, that's the way it is. Sadly, not all families are good, and not all friends are true.

Outside those safe, comfortable surroundings, we must be careful who we believe is speaking truth. Too often the real message is not openly stated, but is hidden by carefully chosen words and manner of presentation. Unless we are careful we

A Match Made In Heaven

can be taken in by those who want something we might not willingly give.

How can we protect ourselves? Must we really be on guard all the time? The short answer to that is, mostly yes. It's okay to engage in those fun exchanges up to the point it becomes clear the other expects us to do something that hasn't been openly discussed. That's when our defenses must go up.

Think of flirting with a pretty young lady or a handsome young man. At some point it becomes clear the other has more than flirting in mind. Unless that is in your mind as well, that's when you should turn on your **personal security system** or expose yourself to potentially unpleasant consequences. Better turn it on anyway until you understand exactly what he/she has in mind for you; it may not be what he/she wants you to think it is.

What's this about a personal security system? Glad you asked, I was just going to tell you. We simply have to ask ourselves a few questions and make sure we have the right answers. But before we get into that, there is one ironclad, never to be ignored rule for important messages: **NEVER LET YOURSELF BE RUSHED INTO** a really important, life-changing decision.

Another thing, if it's a legal matter, especially if there are big bucks involved, get it in writing. I could have sued that dealer if I'd thought to take those records along with the Nash. And make sure you understand exactly what you are signing. If it's complicated, take it to an attorney. *The fool and his money are soon parted. In the multitude of counselors there is safety.*

When pressed for an instant decision, insist on having time to consider the message. When dealing with a door to door salesman, insist that you will let him know your decision the following day. Most will have several reasons why you should decide right now, including possibly, sweetening the offer. Don't be fooled; if he won't come back, show him the door.

Truth & Freedom

There are plenty of reputable businesses near where you live that will sell you a similar product for a similar price, and will be there to help you when it doesn't meet your expectations. I forget that rule sometimes, and a few years ago paid a door-to-door salesman $2,500 for a vacuum cleaner. That's not exactly a life-changing event, but it is something I had determined I would never do and vow I'll never do again.

A Match Made In Heaven

The Personal Security System – Answer these 10 Questions:

1. Is this an appeal to reason or to emotion? If an appeal to emotion, stop right here! This person is manipulating you by short-circuiting the thought process, **switching you from thinking to feeling**. Do not trust manipulators! **Do not make decisions based on emotions!**

2. What is the message? What does this person want me to believe?

3. Is this the whole message? A lot of people have been conned by a perfectly believable message, delivered by an honest looking man or woman, leading to a series of suggestions that ended with them paying big bucks for a promised payoff that never came. Salesmen are trained to ask innocent questions requiring a yes answer, to get you used to saying yes. It's part of their manipulation toolkit.

That's what the vacuum cleaner guy worked on me, and I fell for it. Be wiser than I was; wait for the bottom line, and don't be taken in by psychological tricks.

4. Why does he/she want me to believe that? What is the motive, what's in it for him/her?

5. What does he/she expect me to do in response to the message? Ask the question even if it's obvious. Just asking engages the thinking machinery!

6. What will it cost me? Careful! Cost can be a lot of things besides money.

7. What will I gain from it? Gain, too, can be a lot of things besides money.

8. Will what I get be worth what it costs me? No one else can answer this question for any of us. Part of many come-ons is the challenge to find out for yourself if it's worth it. If you don't know the answer, don't take the bait. Some things you can only give away once.

9. **Why should I trust this person?** How sure am I he/she will follow through with his/her part of the bargain? Is he promising something he can' deliver? What do I know about her track record? Do I **know** he's someone I can trust? Is this her message, or is she fronting for someone else?

10.   **Do I have other information about this person or this offer?** If so, what does that suggest I do?

Again, if you don't know the answers, don't take the bait. If you have other information that sheds light on the message, what does it say about believing the message or trusting the messenger?

That's the Personal Security System. It can help you make good decisions about acting on suggestions, even if it is not a failsafe security system. And don't overlook the fact that it is really helpful in analyzing propaganda as well.

Only when we understand exactly what's expected from us, why that person wants that from us, what it will cost and what we will get in exchange, should we accept others' suggestions. Many an old sailor (this old sailor not one of them, thankfully) has a story of having followed a pretty young thing to her house for a party only to wake up in an alley hours later wearing only his skivvies and dog tags, barefoot, lost and broke. The lucky ones were knocked out early in the encounter, so didn't take home a parting gift they absolutely did not want and had not bargained for.

It's hard to protect ourselves from outcomes like those when we're full of booze or other mood altering substance. Self protection is the best possible motive for being choosey about whom we hang out with and what we eat, drink, etc., when

A Match Made In Heaven

with them. One thing my Dad drummed into his kids – you have to watch out for yourself. No one else cares (not even close to the expression he used) what happens to you, no matter what they say.

It's really hard for us guys (and you gals) to protect ourselves when we're looking into a pair of laughing, let's do it eyes, especially if those eyes are in a pretty/handsome face, and that face is above what looks to be a better than average body. Who's got time for silly questions at times like that? Especially after imbibing as above?

Protection from that kind of temptation is a good reason for committing to one person, for life, and for staying out of bars and night clubs when away from home, wife and kids. What you're looking at may promise more excitement than you have at home, but if you commit to the ones at home you are a lot less likely to end up with the kind of excitement you really don't want or need.

I've been talking about the kind of message that can get us into big trouble in a hurry. Other messages – some obvious, some hidden – can just chip away at us, our person, our property, our money. The obvious scams are the easiest to deal with. Just ask the questions, make sure we know everything we'll get and all it'll cost, and if we can't trust the messenger, get out of there!

Let's look now at one example of the deceptive, insidious messages that can slowly drain the life out of us, **those no-annual-fees, no-transfer-fee credit card offers we get in the mail**.

1. **Is this an appeal to reason or to emotion?** Actually it's intended to play on my desire to get a happier life by reducing my charge card payments. Probably, unless I am really desperate, understand the cost, and am willing to pay the piper down the road, I should stop right here.

2. **What's the message?** Transferring my credit card debt to this card will give me that extra money I need to get out of debt, live from day to day, etc.

3. **Is this the whole message, or just the lead in to another one?** You can't tell without more information. Remember to watch for a change in message as the pitch progresses.

4. **Why does the bank want me to believe that?** So I'll switch cards and become a customer/victim, preferably for life. The bank doesn't care about the customer part – what it wants is your money.

5. **What action does he/she expect me to take in response to the message?** Just sign the contract and transfer any other card balances to this one.

6. **What's it going to cost me?** They say it costs nothing, but unless I am careful, lots of money for a very long time.

7. **What will I get out of it?** For now a little breathing room and a little extra cash to use as I please, but that can lead to a lifetime of debt slavery unless I can get out of its clutches.

8. **Will what I get be worth what it costs?** No one but me can answer that question for me.

9. **Why should I trust this company?** I shouldn't! It's not my friend. I didn't ask it for help; it came to me. I should be suspicious of its motives.

10. **Do I have other information that sheds light on this message?** If not, where can I go to find it?

That kind of offer is easy to see through once we've seen what happens to those who bite. Much more insidious and even more evil are **hidden** messages designed to get us to change to – or cling to – a lifestyle that benefits others at our expense. Obvious examples are television shows and movies presented as

A Match Made In Heaven

entertainment that include nonverbal suggestions that we do something we are not naturally inclined to do. Or to reinforce behavior we are engaging in but know we shouldn't be.

A historical example of this kind of hidden message is found in forties and fifties era movies where cigarettes and booze were everywhere. All the good guys and not so good gals light up at every opportunity, and indulge in a drink or two in whatever situation they find themselves. The nonverbal message – *This is the way people behave in this kind of situation.*

I've tried to deal with losing my true love by drinking a lot of booze. Have you? Did it help? Not for me it didn't! I just ended up spending a lot of money and adding a headache and queasy stomach to everything else I was dealing with!

We'd like to think those hidden suggestions were put into those movies for some artistic reason. In truth, the producers were paid handsomely for showcasing everything from a particular brand of cigarette to a particular model of car. **And you should not think communicators today aren't paid well for suggesting those life style changes they keep pushing!** They are part of a marketing (aka, propaganda) campaign designed with the viewers as targets.

But it's not just in entertainment we must watch for these insidious, freedom stealing messages. An even greater evil is the ever increasing distortions by what once were trusted news outlets. We'll look later at some of the methods propagandists use to deceive us by controlling the news and forming the opinions of those who trust the media. For now let's look at an actual example of slanted journalism, current as I typed the first draft of this chapter, – an opinion piece from the Hartford, Connecticut, Courant. Please read it through then use your Personal Security System to decide whether you should believe either the author or the publisher.

Truth & Freedom

Birthers make up the extreme right wing of the extreme right wing of the extremely right wing right wingers.

You just can't get any farther out on the fringes than these folks and still be able to dip a toe in reality.

Birthers make the people who feared the "New World Order," and saw black government helicopters everywhere seem almost normal. Actually, these folks are of a similar mindset, only the conspiracy theory has changed.

That theory is: President Obama was born in Kenya, not Hawaii, and as such is not eligible to be president of the United States.

No matter how much proof is produced, no matter how many copies of Obama's birth certificate they see, no matter how many court cases they lose (all of them), Birthers cannot be dissuaded from this one-way trip into la-la land.

Given that Birthers are like members of the conspiracy theorists all-star team, I can kind of understand why they might not be convinced by legal documents. Forgeries all, right?

But what I don't understand is how they rationalize the birth announcements that appeared in Hawaii newspapers right after Obama was born?

On Aug. 13 and 14, 1961, Obamas birth notice was published in both the Honolulu Advertiser and the Honolulu Star-Bulletin listing the home address of his parents.

"Were the state Department of Health and Obama's parents really in cahoots to give false information to the newspapers, perhaps intending to clear the way for the

A Match Made In Heaven

baby to someday be elected president of the United States?"" the Star-Bulletin asked sarcastically in a 2009 editorial.

Well, from the Birthers' perspective, "exactly."

I bring this up because we may have just had our first significant Birther sighting in Connecticut.

A Republican state senator from Danbury named Michael McLachlan has introduced a bill in the legislature that would require candidates for president and vice president to prove they are natural-born citizens.

McLachlan told The Courant's Chris Keating "I don't consider this a Birther bill. I believe this is a presidential qualification bill. I'm taking it right out of the Constitution. It is very simple."

Right.

McLachlan is pretty conservative for Connecticut. He's big on the Constitution, suspicious of the federal government, a nonbeliever in church-state separation and an opponent of "Obamacare."

Although McLachlan's actions certainly can be interpreted otherwise, I'm not sure he is in direct communication with the Birther mothership.

His motivation, I think, is more ideological than delusional, more a part of a concerted effort by Conservatives nationwide to defeat Obama in 2012 by denying him a place on the ballot in some states.

The Arizona legislature is soon expected to pass a bill that would set a strict standard for proving natural citizenship for presidential candidates. Similar efforts are

Truth & Freedom

underway in other red states such as Missouri, Texas, Georgia and Montana.

And who would decide if the candidate's documentation was valid? The secretary of state, who in a red state would most likely be a Republican secretary of state, which could mean, well: Where have you gone, Katherine Harris?

Such rulings could throw the presidential election results into chaos. Would disqualifications by individual states be constitutional? Could the U. S. Supreme Court end up deciding another presidential election?

There is no chance McLachlan's bill will be enacted in Connecticut.

I base this assumption on the fact that the State Sen. Gayle Slossberg, co-chairwoman of the committee where the bill was filed, called it "ridiculous."

Nice try, though.

Now, whatever your personal position on the issue may be please reread this article assuming this opinion piece appeared in your daily paper and was directed at you, then think about what you've read there and write down your answers to the Security System questions. I won't grade you on your answers. I'm not here to tell anyone what he should believe, or whom he should trust to be telling him the truth. My task is to teach you to make those decisions for yourself.

Here are the questions. Please write down your answers before looking at the page where I'll record mine. The idea is not to get the same answers I did, but to get a feel for why I came to the answers I did.

Is this an appeal to reason or to emotion?

A Match Made In Heaven

What is the message?

Is this the whole message, or just the lead in to another one?

Why does he/she want me to believe that?

What action does he/she expect me to take in response to the message?

What's it going to cost me?

What will I get out of it?

Will what I get be worth what it costs?

Why should I trust this person?

Do I know of other information that sheds light on this message? If so, what does that tell me about believing the message?

Here are my answers to the questions. Yours will surely be different, depending on your background, your knowledge of political systems and procedures, and what you already believe is true. As I said above, these are decisions you have to make for yourself. No one else can make them for you.

Is this an appeal to reason or to emotion? Clearly it's an appeal to emotion. Very little information is given and virtually all of that consists of deliberate falsifications, aka lies.

What is the message? A small group of extreme right wing nut cases are mounting a foolish effort to bar Barrack Obama from running for reelection in 2012. Plus, the good, liberal, right minded populace of (my state) will not allow this charade to be played out here.

Is this the whole message, or just the lead in to another one? While this article appears to stand alone, it actually is a small part of an ongoing campaign to discourage states from changing their constitutions to make sure candidates for office are legally qualified to hold those offices. Oddly, it seems the writer did not notice that in writing the article he makes it clear he believes Mr. Obama is **not** eligible to be President, or at least is not able to prove he is eligible.

Note too, that being big on the Constitution, suspicious of the federal government, a nonbeliever in church-state separation or an opponent of Obamacare are signs of kookiness. The article is both a distraction, aimed at keeping the reader from wondering if there may be something to *Birther* concerns about Mr. Obama's eligibility and a direct attempt to establish a negative reaction to those who question anything connected with Mr. Obama.

Why does he/she want me to believe that? He is afraid I might believe some of the 'nonsense' the 'Birthers' put out and act differently than I have been programmed to act. He wants to discourage me from looking into the facts concerning eligibility or any of the Obama Administration's offerings.

What action does he/she expect me to take in response to the message? Assuming this appeared in my state, he wants me to be sure to support, vote for and assure the election of non-conservative candidates for state positions. In addition, he may be softening me up for a plea for financial support of actions against red state moves that would deny Mr. Obama the presidency in 2012.

What's it going to cost me? Blindly obeying the call to support any cause or action without fully understanding its real objectives is a recipe for being enslaved in one way or another. So, I'll give up a whole lot I don't want to give up.

What will I get out of it? Nothing good. If people of this mindset acquire the power to prevent such actions, the

A Match Made In Heaven

Constitution and the rights enumerated in it may as well not exist.

Will what I get be worth what it costs? You're kidding, right?

Why should I trust this person? I shouldn't! I never trust anyone I know is lying to me.

Do I know of other information that sheds light on this message? If so, what does that tell me about believing the message? I have information as I type this today I didn't have when I wrote the first draft. Recently a court in Georgia heard evidence showing that 1) one must be a "natural born citizen" to be eligible to be president, 2) Supreme court rulings were cited as establishing as legal precedent that "natural born" means born to parents both of whom were citizens of this country at the time of ones birth and 3) evidence provided by Mr. Obama himself shows that his father was never a citizen of this country, but at the time of Obama's birth was a British citizen. Failure to appear and defend against the allegations made against his eligibility amounts to tacit agreement with the plaintiffs that he is not eligible, and/or knows he cannot prove he is eligible.

Nothing in the *Courant* article addresses any of these issues, and therefore it should be treated with utmost indifference

[Neither Mr. Obama nor his attorney appeared in court to challenge the allegations, so you'd think the Judge should have ruled in favor of the plaintiffs. Instead, he without explanation, ruled for the defendants, a ruling later upheld by a higher court. The *Courant* article was partially right in stating that all lawsuits challenging eligibility lost. What he didn't tell us is that up to that time, no case had actually been tried, all having been dismissed because the plaintiffs "lacked standing", even though one plaintiff actually had been a candidate for the presidency in 2008.]

Truth & Freedom

We can get a good feeling for whether we should believe such messages by using our Personal Security System, in fact, it should be our first line of defense. Its power for unraveling this kind of message increases as we get more information from as many sources as possible. Careful though, one author I recently read recommended taking the "middle position" of a number of opinion sources. Given the omnipresence of the single minded Managed Media of today, that is a sure recipe for being deceived.

People who pull this kind of scam count on our being too busy with entertainment, sports and computer games, and too involved in things needing immediate attention, to dig out the information. And if they think we aren't all that busy, they'll create events, scandals, crises, threats, etc., sufficient to assure we stay busy. If we want to protect ourselves, if we want to live as free people, we must do the work. We must be very careful in deciding whom we trust to tell us the truth.

Another thing – we can't depend on *experts*. Experts become known as experts by being called experts by others who think the same way the expert thinks. [Kind of sounds like the *Courant* article, doesn't it?!] Often those are the very ones who indoctrinated that person in whatever subject they say he is expert in.

Experts tend to make their living by selling their expertise. How can we be sure an expert is telling the truth? John Grisham lawyer novels sometimes have one side hiring the testimony of an expert and the other side hiring its own expert to counter that expert's expert opinions. Sadly, there is no dependable way, short of extensive research beyond our own personal experience, for us to know which, if either, is telling the truth.

On the other hand, there are people who do have knowledge we don't have and who back up their opinions with information we can check about how and why they came to those opinions, people whose opinions we can trust. Beware the "expert" (or

A Match Made In Heaven

editor, or politician) who states an opinion without backing it up with information you can check for yourself! And remember Ronald Reagan's slogan, "Trust but verify!"

I realize what I've given you here is not a perfect security system. At best, it can help you decide who to trust for the information you believe and by believing store in your RAM. I will explore with you a much more powerful method for determining truth in the next three chapters. Regretfully, applying that method requires more time and effort than is appropriate for moderately important questions like what car to buy or whom you should trust to take your teenage daughter to the prom.

Truth & Freedom
A Few Fallacies Commonly Used in Propaganda

The *Courant* article above is a propaganda piece potentially much more dangerous than a stranger's pitch trying to get you to do something that will benefit him/her at your expense. Before leaving this chapter, I will give you some tools you can use to help you recognize propaganda. **Knowing you are the target of a propaganda attack is the essential first step to protecting yourself from it.**

I present below a collection of tools for identifying propaganda adapted from a Free Republic posting of several years ago. If we are to protect ourselves properly, we must have a much wider and deeper understanding of the propagandist's purposes and techniques than presented there. To start you on the path to gaining that understanding, I've copied here (with permission) the Table of Contents from Dr. Brian Anse Patrick's excellent book, ***The Ten Commandments of Propaganda.*** You will find the book's ***Introduction*** in **Appendix I** near the end of this book. In that he details the eleven essentials of an effective propaganda campaign, information you will find most helpful

Table of Contents – *The Ten Commandments of Propaganda*

a. **Control the flow of information**

b. **Reflect the values and beliefs of the audience**

c. **Disambiguate – make distinctions definite and clear**

d. **Use group pressure to horizontally shape beliefs and behavior**

e. **Cognitively penetrate and stick**

f. **Distance the propaganda from the source**

g. **Accommodate informational needs and habits**

A Match Made In Heaven

h.   Address psychological, spiritual and social needs

i.   Personalize and dehumanize as appropriate

j.   Dispense truth, facts, logic and science

k.   Demonstrate good ethics (and don't get caught)

What I mean by the **MM** in what follows is the **Managed Media**; that part of the media that coordinates closely and always presents a bias that is (currently) anti-American, anti-Christian and generally unpatriotic. You'll find this information helpful in spotting bias in media, whatever the source. When we get to the bottom of slanted news, we always find a scheme either to control our actions or take our money – too often, both.

Twenty Ways the Managed Media (MM) Bias News Reports

Bias in the media takes many forms. Here are some of the tactics the MM use to deceive and control. (Note: "Media" is a plural noun, so the abbreviation, MM, is also plural. I have used plural verbs describing what the MM do.) That sounds wrong when you read "MM" as two letter "M"s. If that bothers you, you can either say to yourself, "managed media" or just take your pen and change the verb to one that sounds right to you. (I'm Just Kidding! Especially if you're reading this on Kindle or Nook!)

1. The Lie. Often the MM resort to an outright lie. The lie involves some very specific fact, like a forged memo, false reports of a crowd booing when the crowd actually applauded (or the opposite), false claims that Sandy Berger returned the "original" documents, false attribution of statements to public figures, false charges that American soldiers are targeting journalists, etc. A lie current as I type this is the fake **Certification of Live Birth** touted as proof Mr. Obama is eligible

Truth & Freedom

to be President of the United States, which likely is both a lie and a diversion from the real issue of his citizenship status.

The ultimate goal of telling the lie is that it will be accepted as fact, both influencing what we do and discouraging us from trying to find the truth. "Bush was a draft dodger", "Bush lied", "There is no Social Security crisis", are examples from the 2004 election. We were "treated" to two years of blatant lies prior to that election. Between 2004 and 2008, the MM gave us four years of constant propaganda after seeing their program didn't get the job done in 2004.

The only defense against the lie is knowing truth, which too often is hard to come by.

2. The Memory Hole. The Memory Hole is where the MM hide information they want to keep from us. They simply don't report that certain events occurred and hope no one else will. Because the "news" is managed, if one source uses the Memory Hole, others will too. It sometimes seems that we are in the same situation the Chinese were during the Cultural Revolution – they looked at what the government was **not** reporting to help them understand what was really happening.

The MM don't just fail to report unwanted news, they fill up available space with unimportant sensations. **We protect ourselves against the memory hole by getting our news from as many competing sources as possible.**

3. Ventriloquist journalism. Another tactic the MM use is to insert its opinions into news stories by making it appear it is news that some person has that opinion. Watch for phrases like *critics say, some say, experts say* and realize it's not hard to find someone who'll say on camera or to a reporter, that he holds an opinion the media want us to adopt as our own.

4. Polls. This relative of ventriloquist journalism uses slanted polls in which "the people" are the ones allegedly speaking.

A Match Made In Heaven

The MM slant polls by formatting questions to get the desired response, by selecting the poll participants, and by similar tricks.

An example from several years ago: Eighty-two percent of Americans polled said they would want the feeding tube removed if they were in the same situation as Terri Schiavo, a young woman in a persistent vegetative state but not legally brain dead. The poll questions incorrectly described Ms. Schiavo's condition. A later poll using questions that accurately described her condition found a large majority said the tube should not be removed in that situation.

[This is a good place for exercising our personal security system. Why should those controlling the MM want us to believe most Americans would want to be starved to death or die of thirst when we are no longer able to make our wishes known? Keep in mind, too, that honest polls, the results of which you will never see unless they support "the narrative", are used for testing the effectiveness of propaganda programs.]

Trust no poll unless the results are accompanied by a description of the sample size and makeup, the questions asked and the available responses. Many times the wording of the questions and the choice of available answers are designed to influence how participants respond.

5. Buzzwords. The MM repeat a word or phrase so often that the word takes on a life of its own, giving signposts to focus on for those who pay little attention to the news. "Enron", "Sarah Palin", "racist" "right winger", "homophobe", "Birther" are not arguments in themselves so can't be refuted, but take on the force of argument through repetition.

Protect yourself by asking, "What exactly does this word mean and why is it used here?"

6. **Coordination with candidates.** This is a very old and still much used tactic. An example from the 2004 George W. Bush campaign: CBS timed the release of Dan Rather's fake memo to coincide with the Democrat "fortunate son" campaign. I'm sure you can think of examples from both sides of the political spectrum.

Be aware that simultaneous startling revelations timed to coincide with other news stories and opinion pieces by an assumed competitive media are in fact evidence of collusion to support a "narrative" or to give the media an excuse for not reporting less sensational and potentially undesirable (to their sponsors) happenings.

7. **Smear/personal attack/outrage.** This is another golden oldie. In the 1950's, Edward R. Murrow smeared Joe McCarthy by carefully editing film, a tactic that caused Bobby Kennedy to walk out on a dinner in honor of Murrow because of "what he did to my friend Joe."

In recent years, we have seen so-called "journalists" shout down those with whom they disagree, accuse "9-11" families of "having a good time" while grieving for lost loved ones, and attack the facial features and wardrobe of those who dare take politically incorrect stands. Targets in the Clinton era were Paula Jones and Linda Tripp. More recently, Sarah Palin was among their favorites. They also characterize opponents as rednecks, whackos and stupid knuckle-draggers (currently: Birthers and Tea Partyers). The smear is designed to intimidate the opposition and reinforce stereotypes implanted by other propaganda.

Ask yourself if the shouting, and name calling are part of a reasoned discussion, or are designed to prevent others from presenting their side or making them sound untrustworthy.

8. **Euphemisms.** The MM use euphemisms to downplay otherwise serious stories. In 2013 we still hear of

A Match Made In Heaven

"undocumented immigrants" instead of "illegal aliens" and "insurgents" instead of "terrorists". "Fetus" instead of "unborn child" has been around since the 1960s.

Ask yourself, "What does this word or phrase really mean?"

9. False appearance of evenhandedness. The MM pretend to treat a story evenhandedly, interviewing persons from both sides of the debate but giving only a few seconds to their opponents' side and letting those presenting their side drone on. The MM will interview fringe Republicans who have little to say, or uneducated individuals, for the purpose of discrediting the Republican position. The MM never present a true clash of ideas.

Your only defense is to know the positions of both parties.

10. Opinion as fact. This one is the most common. It puts opinions into news stories instead of on the editorial pages where they belong. This is often done by way of polls and ventriloquist journalism.

11. The race card. A common ploy is to attack the sponsors of any unwanted program by claiming they are racially motivated.

Ask yourself how this fact, if true, impacts the truth of the statements.

12. Issue exclusion/false alternatives. Here we have a marriage of straw man attack (15) and memory hole. The MM present the issue as a choice between two alternatives; a weak, wishy-washy approach is presented as the conservative approach, while the leftist approach is heralded as the only alternative. True conservative proposals are flushed down the memory hole.

Every time the minimum wage becomes an issue, the MM present us the choice of raising the minimum wage by a large amount or a small amount. The MM ignore the economic research that suggests any minimum wage harms the economy.

Truth & Freedom

In the war on terror (or any recent war) the MM present the issue as peace vs. war instead of victory vs. defeat or right vs. wrong.

It is difficult to identify the Straw Man fallacy or the Memory Hole attack unless we are familiar with the issues. Stay Informed!

13. Both sides are guilty. When one of its own is accused of some nefarious crime, the MM are quick to point out the failings of those making the accusation. In the **1990's**, every eruption of Whitewater or Monica-gate resulted in repeated MM references to Thomas Jefferson's slaves or Watergate.

That is why Watergate, a pie in the face of Republican President Richard Nixon, will forever remain a current issue while Whitewater, a Clinton embarrassment, was crammed into the memory hole by MM editors determined to keep it there.

Ask how the guilt of one party absolves another party of guilt.

14. Whitewash/Softball criticism of public figures. Whenever the MM are forced to face some scandal that reflects badly on their own, they pretend to investigate, then criticize the perpetrators for irrelevant and less damaging reasons. The CBS/Dan Rather investigators criticized CBS for trying to be first instead of for false and biased reporting. The MM criticized Bill Clinton for committing adultery and lying instead of for perjury and trading high tech ICBM delivery systems to China. Their softball whitewashes provide cover for the perpetrators of real crimes/faults.

Again, Stay Informed!

15. Straw man arguments. The MM frequently construct a weak, obviously wrongheaded approach to a problem, pretends that's the opposition's approach, and then proceeds to knock its straw man to pieces. This is done in the news pages via

A Match Made In Heaven

ventriloquist journalism, and openly on the editorial pages where almost any opinion is safe from libel suits.

The best defense – ask yourself if any sane person would really suggest such a thing, then ask yourself why the MM want you to believe someone actually did suggest it.

16. Government solution assumption. The MM are overly fond of government solutions – the only solution to any problem is bigger government and higher taxes.

Ask yourself three questions: "Has the big government approach ever worked here or elsewhere?" "Why do those pushing this idea want me to believe it is the best approach to solving the problem?" "Are there private sector alternatives?"

17. The label game. This game, a relative of (8) Euphemisms, is played by attaching positive labels to friends and negative labels to opponents. Persons quoted are experts if they support the MM view or some negative term if they don't. Islamic terrorists are *insurgents, militants, freedom fighters, guerrillas* or *rebels* but never *terrorists*. Illegal aliens are "undocumented immigrants". In the *Courant* example, those who want to make sure candidates for public office are qualified to hold that office are ridiculed by being called "extreme right wingers" and "birthers".

Make it a constant practice to stop reading any writing where this is discovered and vow never to read anything written by that author again.

18. Hypocrisy. The MM will investigate (or invent) Republican scandals while ignoring Democrat scandals. The Swift Boat vets, who held John Kerry to a standard of truth, were vilified while CBS was using Dan Rather's forged document in an attempt to smear President Bush.

Truth & Freedom

It helps to read carefully both sides of such debates, evaluating the believability of both.

19. Scare tactics. The MM present many issues as doomsday events that will destroy the planet, end social security, end school lunches, etc., with Republicans being the culprits who are making these terrible things happen.

As I edit this in February 2013, we are still being bombarded with stories of glaciers melting, polar bears drowning, sea levels rising, etc., etc. "Experts" (and non-expert movie stars and failed politicians) are paraded across the pages of newspapers and on TV news programs, warning us that we are destroying the planet through global warming. Every change in weather patterns is cited as further proof that human caused carbon dioxide is the culprit. The very solid science challenging those extreme statements is completely ignored, the memory hole at work of course.

Again, Stay Informed!

20   Selective editing. This one is hard to spot and very common. Change the camera angle, include film or audio from another context, exclude explanatory comments, etc., and we are given a completely false picture of events. Our only defense against selective editing is getting our news from as many really different sources as we can. Rumsfeld's infamous "We go to war with the army we have" was non-controversial and made perfect sense in the context of his remarks, which the MM tried hard to make sure you would never see. An egregious recent example concerns the Trayvon Martin/George Zimmerman case now scheduled to be tried in June, 2013.

The MM in reporting that case posted side by side pictures of a much younger Martin and an especially damaging mug shot of Zimmerman made years earlier. To the best of my knowledge, no reliable photos of the 17 year old have been published, and current and contemporaneous photos of Zimmerman show a

A Match Made In Heaven

slim clean cut Hispanic man, not the crazed and dazed figure of the earlier photo. This was an unmistakable effort to stir up black anger over the killing of a black 17 year old by a "white" policeman. Who was behind this story, and what his (or their) motive may have been is unknown.

With practice, you can become proficient at spotting the fallacies in the news and opinion pages of your daily paper. It's a lot harder to spot these in television reporting because things move fast and seem to be designed to leave an impression, not to provide information. **And that's a very good reason for insisting you get your news in print.**

Here we have looked at **Logical Fallacies** used in propaganda. Another approach is to look at propaganda through the screen of **Propaganda Techniques**. I've attached as **Appendix II** a list of 52 of those, extracted from a Wikipedia article on Propaganda. You will want to take a look at that list as well.

One technique – the **bandwagon** – obviously applies to an article in my today's (4-5-2013) hometown paper stating that, for the first time, a majority of Americans favor legalization of marijuana. An accompanying graph shows the percentage favoring legalization steadily increases as the younger, already heavily propagandized respondents are added to the mix of responders. The article essentially encourages readers to drop their resistance to legalization, **climb on the bandwagon** and **be on the winning side**, two related propaganda techniques.

The procedure for deciding **WHO** is worth believing is not foolproof because it depends on how accurately we answer a series of questions. It can't establish the truth of a statement, but can help us decide whether we should believe the one making it, so it **is** useful. Think of it as a construction worker's hard hat; it will protect part of you if you wear it. Partial protection is better than no protection, right?

Truth & Freedom

In the next chapter I'll describe a reliable method for deciding **WHAT** is worth believing. What I've presented here is comparable to popping the hood of your car and looking, listening, smelling what's there to get an idea of what, if anything, could be wrong with the engine. Chapter III adds the equivalent of a computerized engine analyzer to the truth seeker's tool kit – a method for establishing the credibility, AKA believability – of a proposition, message or statement. Beside that important application, it can be used for developing ones own understanding of a mass of information.

Before proceeding to the next part of the discussion, you might try applying the Personal Security System to the message of this chapter. I'll provide my answers to the ten questions; your challenge will be deciding whether you should believe I'm being truthful in presenting either the message or my answers.

1. Is this an appeal to reason or to emotion? Mostly to reason, though I have made some statements intended to convince you that knowing truth is essential for remaining free, none of which are here supported by evidence.

2. What is the message? In answering the 10 questions, you engage your reasoning powers to help you avoid falling for the machinations of those who want to control what you do. Learning some of the techniques propagandists use will make you better able to protect your personal wellbeing and your freedom.

3. Is this the whole message, or just the lead in to another one? It's the whole message for this part of the discussion. It's a lead in to the more powerful tool that follows.

4. Why does he/she want me to believe that? I see forces working in our society and all over the world to take away our freedoms and enslave us to unseen masters. This chapter, and this book are my effort to gain partners in the struggle for freedom. If you who read this are determined to be free, that

A Match Made In Heaven

makes it much easier for others of like mind to succeed in becoming free.

5. What action does he/she expect me to take in response to the message? Hopefully you will learn how to avoid acting on messages intended to enslave you in one way or another.

6. What's it going to cost me? The small price of this book and the effort needed to learn and apply the discipline the method requires.

7. What will I get out of it? Hopefully a more satisfying life.

8. Will what I get be worth what it costs? Only you can answer that question.

9. Why should I trust this person? You know nothing about me except that I've written this book, so you have every reason to question my motives for writing it. It will help if you will think carefully about the message and decide for yourself if it is intended to free you to pursue what's good for you or to trick you into advancing someone else's agenda.

10. Do I know of other information that sheds light on this message? If so, what does that tell me about believing the message? I don't know what you know, so can't answer this question. It's always helpful to spend an appropriate amount of time and effort to check out any message aimed at changing ones behavior.

Let me add a couple of afterthoughts here. I have made disparaging remarks about experts and others who share their opinions with us. I do not want to give you the idea that you should never trust anyone, but to warn you that many "experts" make statements not necessarily based on logic and solid research. Some, for unknown reasons, do so to sell us on some false idea they may or may not know is false.

Truth & Freedom

And I've either ignored emotions in this discussion or presented them as unworthy motivators to action. There is no denying that emotions can and do drive us to act. Often those actions are beneficial, but they can be extremely harmful. The problems arise when strong emotions completely take over, shorting out the rational, decision-making part of the brain.

Think of your brain as a computer and a strong emotion as a glitch that takes over and makes it do odd things. Emotions in themselves are a necessary and wonderful part of being human. It's when anger turns to wrath, hunger to gluttony, desire to lust, fear to panic, dislike to detestation, that emotions take control – far too often with disastrous results.

I know of no way for the non-Christian to defend against those disasters other than by adopting the Stoic approach to life, rigorously beating down all emotion, like Star Trek's Spock doing only what is rational and reasonable. Having tried living that life for several years, I can attest that it is pretty much free of emotion-related problems. That freedom came at the price of giving up nearly all pleasures except the feeling of satisfaction that came from knowing my way of life was far superior to that of other mortals. (In short, I don't recommend it!)

The Christian has many weapons to use against those powerful urges to do what is not in his best interest to do. Supreme among his weapons is the desire and determination to emulate Jesus Christ in praying constantly. The commitment to prayer is supported by the commandments to love God with ones whole being and to love ones neighbor as himself.

His Helper, the Holy Spirit, not only guides, teaches and rebukes, but also provides the fruit of the Spirit – love, joy, peace, patience, kindness, goodness, gentleness, faithfulness and self control. He has available God's armor which enables him to stand victorious in every battle. Christians have no excuse for being controlled by runaway emotions.

A Match Made In Heaven
CHAPTER III.

The TruthAlyzer

How Can I Decide What to Believe

In this chapter we will look at two different situations, deciding for yourself what to believe by evaluating available evidence, and deciding whether to accept someone else's ideas about what you should believe. Both will use the process I employed over the years to develop information published in 40+ technical papers, several of which received "best paper" awards. The method has very wide application, from evaluating propaganda to developing a theory about a crime scene, to determining truths about the most important things in life.

Unless we know we have all the evidence pro or con – that seldom happens in the real world – we can never be absolutely sure we know the truth. At best we can make a decision on the evidence that's available, and if there is too much available, on the evidence we can adequately process in a reasonable time. When we use only part of the evidence, the process shows what is **likely** to be true and worth believing.

It's a simple procedure, consisting of nine steps. Using the "engine analyzer" analogy of the last chapter, the nine steps are the programming software and your brain is the computer.

The Nine Steps:

1. Identify and record the question to be answered or the problem to be solved. This will help you stay focused on the task at hand and make it easier to explain to others exactly what you have done.

2. Briefly summarize the current status of other investigations aimed at answering the question or solving the problem.

3. Record the data sources, initial assumptions and axioms that will guide the investigation. This is a crucial step, which if done carelessly or without sufficient thought, can lead one far astray.

4. Search a sub-set of the available information until you find enough information to suggest an answer to the question or solution to the problem. Record that answer as the initial working hypothesis. Summarize the reasons you think it may be the solution.

5. Continue exploring the information, looking for evidence that confirms or contradicts the working hypothesis. Record that information, and whether it is supporting or contradictory.

6. Modify the working hypothesis, if necessary, to accommodate any substantial contradictory evidence. Record modified hypotheses using appropriate identifiers, for example, by numbering them as you adopt them. Continue exploring the information, looking for evidence that confirms or contradicts the working hypothesis. Record that information, and whether it is supporting or contradictory.

7. Repeat step 6 exploring information not yet considered until a substantial portion of the available information has yielded significant evidence confirming the latest working hypothesis while revealing no contradictory information. Record this as your answer to the question or solution to the problem.

8. Report in an appropriate medium the final hypothesis, verified by your research to be an answer worth believing to the question or solution of the problem. Include a summary of how you reached your answer or solution, sufficiently detailed that other investigators can understand what you did, why you did it that way, and how you came to your final conclusions.

A Match Made In Heaven

9. Preserve the records of all this. You will need them later to answer questions about your conclusions or your methods.

You have arrived at your position by applying a clearly defined process, utilizing evidence from sources you have identified, and you have detailed how you reached that position. Do not allow yourself to be moved off that position by any lesser process than the one you used to reach it. Trust me, those who do not like your conclusions will use every trick to discredit you, refute you and confuse you and anyone else who adopts your position.

That outlines the method for deciding what to believe. In Chapter IV I will show how to apply the method in developing a hypothesis, there a believable Christian doctrine. If you are averse to the Christian message, please do not let that discourage you from following the discussion. I'm not trying to convert you; I chose to use that project as an example because the evidence is readily available to all and limited to what's in the canonic scriptures and therefore complete and not subject to unexpected future discoveries.

In Chapter V, I will present an example showing how to test an existing doctrine. I chose a Christian doctrine for that example for the same reasons – the evidence is contained in the canonic scriptures, and is not subject to change. For now I will tell you why we need this procedure and give you additional criteria for using it.

I'm sure you are by now scratching your head and wondering if it's ever worth going to all that work to decide what to believe. Let's talk about that for a bit.

We've already agreed – I hope – that we must know what's true if we are to be free to act in ways that advance our own interests instead of someone else's. We can't live as free men and women otherwise. Chapter two presented suggestions for deciding who we should believe. That imperfect tool is all we have when faced with decisions where we don't have the time, resources or desire to use this more powerful tool.

Here we are not dealing with trivial questions where we can live with occasional imperfect or bad decisions. When faced with the really gut-wrenching issues of life, we must decide for ourselves what to believe. We can't leave those decisions to others; we must somehow decide them for ourselves.

Why must we decide for ourselves, you're asking? That's a big question. The short answer is that we can't trust anyone who tells us how to live will have our interests in mind. It's a rare person who will do anything for anyone that doesn't help himself in the process. With those who make their living telling others what to do, helping themselves is the important thing; "helping" others is simply a means to the end of promoting themselves.

I can imagine the gears grinding right now; you're wondering, "Okay, big shot, why are you telling me all this stuff? What's in it for you?"

First, I don't make my living telling anybody what to do. I'm retired, and I made my living and earned my retirement money by applying the process I described above to help others do important things they needed to do. If this book sells well, I will make some money off the sales but it cannot possibly be enough to compensate me for the time and effort that went into writing this book. It's money I don't really need, and that's not what drives me to write these things.

Second, I firmly believe having free people, freely agreeing together on how they will address mutual problems, leads to a much safer, happier, cleaner and all round better world to live in than any other system ever devised. So, yes, there is an element of self interest here, but it cannot be advanced without advancing every honest person's self interest at the same time.

A Match Made In Heaven

Third, the world is full of good, honest people who do things because it's just right to do them. The One whose example I follow as best I'm able has shown what that means by His own example, and He urges all who follow Him to live that way. So, you see, I'm writing this for you because it's right for me and right for you.

That was a bit of a digression; what I was saying is that the world is full of professionals trying mightily to get good honest people to live the way they want them to live. To them, the "**right** way" is any way that helps the manipulators get **their** way. We can never trust such people to tell us what's best for us to do.

We all know a politician or a used car salesman will say anything, promise everything he thinks will close the deal for him. But it's becoming abundantly clear we should not trust even the institutions Americans have always trusted to be truth tellers, to be "on our side". Such institutions include the print, screen and other media whose behavior over the past many years shows they have sold out to the highest bidder. Sadly, that also is true of many in academia and in the sciences.

Let's pick on scientists here. Some scientists claim to have **THE TRUTH** because they've applied the scientific method to whatever they're investigating. What they don't want us to know is the scientific method, even when applied diligently and honestly, cannot determine **THE TRUTH** about anything. At best it can help make sense of the information available; **all its pronouncements are subject to nullification if and when someone discovers evidence never imagined to exist.**

And even more sadly, there's no guarantee a scientist will honestly report what he discovers. Too many scientists bend the truth, hiding unfavorable evidence so their funding will keep coming and their reputations as experts will not be challenged. Recently climate scientist were discovered to have done all the above, adding to that their conspiracy to prevent opposing conclusions from being reviewed or if they succeeded in being reviewed, accepted for publication in "respectable" journals.

Even if we could trust what the scientists and experts tell us they believe is true, the fact is, we can't be absolutely sure scientists have the truth about anything. French and British thinkers proved that several hundred years ago. Even so, the scientific method is the best approach ever discovered for coming close to truth. The process I'm presenting here is just a simplified application of the scientific method.

If we can't be sure we know truth, what's left? How can we direct our lives, how can we live in freedom, if we don't know truth? I answer those two questions by telling you that we – all of us, no exceptions – act upon what we **believe** to be true. If you think about that a bit, you'll see that is true. (Sounds like a contradiction, doesn't it, but there **is** such a thing as self-evident truth.)

That's why so many spend so much time and effort trying to make us believe what they want us to believe. If they control what we believe, they control what we do. If they control enough of what we believe, then we become no better than slaves, doing what benefits them instead of us and those we love. If we are to avoid that kind of "voluntary" slavery, we must somehow learn to decide for ourselves what we will believe.

How do we come to believe enough to decide to act? You must understand that we do decide one way or the other, whether we think it through or not. We all make life-impacting decisions every day, on insufficient and too often erroneous information, acting on beliefs we don't even realize we hold.

You must understand that this is a personal decision. We cannot let anyone make that kind of decision for us. **We'll make that our first criterion** for seriously considering any suggestion

A Match Made In Heaven

that we act in any certain way – **we will consider acting on a suggestion only if it is personally relevant; that is, it will significantly impact our own lives.**

I'm talking about here any communication in any form from anyone who wants to influence what we do, how we act. Obvious examples are the commercials we are bombarded with each hour of every day. Less obvious is the propaganda carefully designed to influence our outlook, controlling how we look at ourselves and our world, and thus controlling what we do.

Let's give these communications, these suggestions, a name. Let's call any communication or suggestion intended to directly or indirectly influence how we act a **motivator.**

We've agreed we'll only concern ourselves with communications – motivators – that are personally relevant. And obviously, we should not take seriously any motivator we don't find believable – credible is the highbrow word. **We'll make credibility our second criterion for considering a motivator. A motivator is credible only if it is internally consistent.** That means it must be logically sound, not containing contradictions or faulty logic.

In chapter II, I showed some ways the media slant the news to trick us into doing what we wouldn't do if we knew the truth. That list is only a subset of logical fallacies. You can find several other useful lists just by Googling Logical Fallacies. Motivators that contain fallacies are worthless. They are inconsistent internally, and are not worth considering. If they contain knowingly constructed fallacies, they are downright pernicious.

And too, **we'll consider a motivator credible only if it is externally consistent**. External consistency has two components –there must be substantial evidence external to the motivator that is **consistent** with the motivator being true. And most importantly, there must be no external evidence **inconsistent** with the motivator being true – evidence that cannot exist if the motivator is true. In testing credibility, we must look for both positive and negative evidence. Ignoring any relevant evidence is foolish; it's a way of lying to oneself, and you know where lies lead us.

We must avoid two things: We must not postpone making a credibility decision until we've evaluated all the evidence because we can never be sure we have all the evidence. At some point, the accumulation of positive and absence of negative evidence should lead us to a credibility decision. If we find solid contradictory evidence we must consider the motivator to be not credible.

And we must not be too quick in deciding a motivator is credible. There are no hard and fast rules about how much supporting evidence makes a proposition credible. Assuming other independent sources of evidence are available, we must look at evidence from a reasonable sample of them, and we must be sure we get an adequate sample from each source.

Only our own gut can tell us when we've seen enough evidence to decide a motivator is credible. Remember, though, once you make public your decision, those who don't like it will be frantically looking for negative evidence you overlooked. We can't wait till we've seen all the evidence, but let's not be like the archeologist who hypothesizes a whole new species based on a single tooth unlike any he's seen before.

Let's review where we are in this process:

1. We won't take seriously anything that will not impact our own lives in some way important to us personally.

2. We won't take seriously any statement that contains logical fallacies.

3. We will consider credible only motivators for which we have solid supporting evidence.

A Match Made In Heaven

4. We will reject as incredible any motivator for which we have solid evidence that could not exist if the motivator's statements were true.

Once we've collected credible supporting evidence, additional supporting evidence of the same kind, from the same source has decreasing value. Think of it this way, if the first bit of evidence has value **1**, and the second, value **1/2**, the tenth, value **1/10**, the **100**th, value **1/100,** any bit of supporting evidence contributes little after the first **20** bits or so. On the other hand, any theory can be destroyed by just one solid piece of evidence that is incompatible with the theory being true.

A word of warning; **an opinion is not evidence.** Opinions are at best conclusions someone has formed about the meaning of evidence, given too-often-unstated assumptions that person accepts as true. Don't even think of accepting another's opinions until you've seen his assumptions, the evidence and the chain of reasoning that led to the opinion. If the assumptions are not reported, if evidence is not provided, if you are not allowed to see the evidence, or if the chain of reasoning is not clear, you must assume the "opinion" was crafted to manipulate and deceive you.

Okay, we're agreed that we'll only consider motivators that are relevant and credible; what do we do when faced with competing relevant, credible and mutually exclusive motivators? Each tells us believing and acting as it suggests will maximize our happiness and well being. They are both credible, but we cannot know for sure that either is true. How do we decide between the two?

That question introduces our third criterion – our criterion for choosing between competing messages. **We should believe the relevant, credible motivator that, if true, will maximize our current and future well being**. By well being I mean physical security, bodily and emotional health, sense of worth, peace of mind, everything each of us personally needs for a long and happy life.

Let's give this criterion a name – we'll say we will accept and act upon the proposition that we find has **maximum personal utility.** This criterion is personally defined – no one can define it for us. Decisions about personal utility almost always involve external evidence.

For our purposes, we will acknowledge that ultimately we can control only our own actions, that only we can choose what's best for us, that we can't choose what's best for anyone else, and that we can freely choose actions we believe will be personally beneficial. (We are speaking of free, responsible adults here.) None of which should be understood as meaning we will benefit from ignoring external realities, including those imposed on us by persons who have power over us.

The hard part of deciding what to believe is creating a valid message from the available information. Deciding that an existing motivator is credible is far easier; we need only check the reliability of positive evidence offered in its support and look for substantial evidence not compatible with the message. I'll give an example of that kind of investigation in Chapter V.

Here I'll demonstrate how to decide between two competing motivators. I'll assume you've done the work to establish that each of two motivators is credible and relevant, and I will provide a greatly oversimplified example showing how to choose between them. I've contrived a shootout between a simplified form of a proposition called Pascal's Wager and a much simplified expression of a message derived from Darwinian evolution. Boiling a message down to a simple statement is a lot more difficult than I've made it appear here, but that must be done before you can make the test. Here goes:

We must decide between two credible and relevant motivators briefly described as follows:

A Match Made In Heaven

The Bible Message – The Bible contains a message from the Creator God to mankind, promising those who act in accordance with that message happiness in this life and after death a happy eternity with him in Heaven.

Evolution's Message – There is no god and no creator. All life evolved from the primeval slime. Man is merely the animal that finds itself currently at the top of the evolutionary chain. Death ends it all, so each person should act in whatever way he or she thinks will prolong life, maximize pleasure and minimize pain. Only the fittest will pass their genes to future generations.

Independent evidence – Scientific studies have credibly shown that those who act in accordance with the Bible Message produce at least as many offspring, are at least as happy, and live at least as long as those who do not.

The messages are mutually exclusive –we cannot believe and act on both at the same time.

The "independent evidence" is important because – if it exists – it shows the **worst** the Bible-Message-believer can expect from his choice is **at least as good as** the **best** the Evolution-Message-believer can expect from his choice. For the purposes of the example we will assume there is such evidence.

A reasonable person will believe and act upon the message that promises **a best outcome much better, and a worst outcome no worse** than, the other **message's best outcome.** He gives up nothing and gains for himself at best a promised result of immeasurable value, and at worst the same result he'd have obtained had he chosen otherwise. Given that we have determined that the two messages are credible and personally relevant, all that remains is to investigate and make a decision about the quality of the Independent Evidence cited above.

If we include in the Bible message the promise of an eternity of torment in Hell for those who do not act in accordance with the message, then the Independent Evidence is irrelevant. The choice then becomes choosing between a message whose **worst outcome** is that there is **no God**, and a message whose **best outcome** is that there is **no God**. That choice is a no-brainer.

That brings us to the bottom line in any decision leading to action – cost vs. benefit. What will this decision cost me, and how much will it benefit me? Is the cost greater than the benefit? If so, I should look for another way of reaching whatever goal I am pursuing. The weakness of Darwinian Evolution for Christians is that it requires giving up something they find precious and comforting and provides no benefit for doing so.

If a motivator's benefit is greater than its cost, and if we know of no better way of achieving our goal, then we should make our decision and act on it. If the opposite is true, we should look elsewhere. As long as we can freely choose what we will do, we can drop one course of action and choose a better one when it comes along. Remember though, decisions lead to actions, and actions have consequences, some of them unpleasant.

But How Can I Know I know the Truth?

So far we've looked at how to know if we should trust someone to be telling the truth, and how to choose between two competing versions of truth. In both I have assumed we should always choose the way of believing that will be best for us in the long run. This is an important criterion for choosing, and really is the only defensible one.

Many if not all of us have been taught that there are situations where one should give up his own benefit or welfare on behalf of another. This too, is good, and society would soon morph into a jungle if this principle were to be abandoned. I want to

A Match Made In Heaven

emphasize here that a free man freely chooses what he will do; he can't let others determine that for him.

But a free man will inevitably be faced with situations where it is in his **long term** interest to advance another's interests at the expense of his **current** interests. This is fundamental to civilized society, and it is the ultimate motivator for the Christian. We freely choose to put off perceived present gain in anticipation of greater future gain. Were it not so, no one would ever choose to do so unless he had been brainwashed – propagandized – into thinking that he was acting in his own interests.

And that brings us – finally – to the subject of this subchapter; "How can I know I know the truth?" The simple answer is that one can rarely – some would say never – be **sure** they know the truth.

Charles Sanders Peirce, (pronounced "purse") founder of American Pragmatism, saw the search for truth to be a series of experiments using a method similar to the one I describe in this chapter. While one cannot be sure the experiment results in truth, he can be confident that he has a credible answer to the question investigated. *"Peirce held the view that truth is immutable and infinity is real, which set him apart from other pragmatists such as William James and John Dewey."* (From: http://en.wikipedia.org/wiki/Pragmatism#Origins, which I hope you will read in its entirety. There you will find such gems as, *"According to the classical pragmatists, knowledge is always shaped by human interests, and the administrator's focus on 'outcomes' simply advances their own interest, but that this focus on outcomes often undermines their citizen's interests, which often are more concerned with process."*)

Repeating the process using other information may produce a credible answer different from the first one. If the answers are not in conflict, one does not negate the other; the combined answer provides an answer "closer" to truth. In Peirce's view, this is an infinite process that theoretically brings one close enough to truth that he may reliably accept it as truth. A good example from Physics is Isaac Newton's Laws of Motion, which accurately describe the interactions between nearly all physical bodies but are inadequate when applied to very small bodies.

In the kind of search I will introduce in the next chapter, we will be dealing with a body of information. Normally, these are "open" collections of facts for the simple fact that we can never be sure we have all the information. If we don't, then information may sometime be found that couldn't exist if what we had taken as truth really were true. That would invalidate our conclusion, and we'd have to replace it with another.

In the example of chapter IV, though, we will be working with a "closed" source of information, the Bible. It is closed because its contents were decided nearly **2000** years ago. Other, conflicting, information may exist, and may even be known, but that is irrelevant to the questions we will address in the example, namely, "What does the Bible teach about this?"

In this case and similar ones, we can know we know the true answer to the question, but that may not bring us any closer to ultimate truth. To test whether this is ultimate truth, we must search external sources for substantial information that conflicts with our answer. If we find none, that establishes our answer as provisionally true; if we do find conflicting information, our answer cannot be true.

What I am interested in here, and what you should be too, is what we need to know in order to make decisions that will be to our long term benefit. When a pit bull comes at one on the street, he doesn't stand there wondering if it is a friendly dog. That's the kind of real world situation I am dealing with in this book.

And that's the final answer to the question of this subchapter. We can't know we know the truth except in those cases where we have done the work of finding it. But we can know we know

A Match Made In Heaven

enough of the truth to keep us out of trouble in our world. Whether what we know is sufficiently accurate to save us from being gnawed by dogs will only be answered as we face the pit bull and act upon what we think we know.

Current conventional wisdom is that there **is** no absolute truth; all truth is relative. This corrosive idea came from fellow Pragmatist William James' perversion of Peirce's statement about belief: *"Do not ask a person what he believes, but observe what he does. His actions reveal what he believes."* (This is a paraphrase, not a direct quote.) Because we all act on what we believe to be true, James took that to mean truth is relative to the mental state of the believer at any given time. This false idea provides moral cover for propagandists and other manipulators who see themselves as not really lying, but as only helping others firm up their beliefs.

I must add a word of caution here – none of what's presented in this chapter should be looked at as a machine into which anyone can just pour information and crank out a credible answer. In developing and reporting the method and the applications that will follow, I learned that it not only takes a lot of hard work and harder thought, I was successful only when I consistently asked for help from the Holy Spirit.

I am confident in predicting any other approach to finding God's truth will yield only nonsense and confusion. Whether the same applies to secular investigations is for someone else to determine.

The concept is simple, but applying it to serious questions may result in an unacceptably large recording effort. For that reason it often makes sense to break down the question or the problem into smaller, easier managed sub-problems, starting with the ones that must first be answered if you are to determine the true answer to the question or solution to the problem.

Truth & Freedom

I'll close this chapter with John Donne's famous poem as a reminder not to take ourselves too seriously.

> *No man is an island,*
> *Entire of itself.*
> *Each is a piece of the continent,*
> *A part of the main.*
> *If a clod be washed away by the sea,*
> *Europe is the less.*
> *As well as if a promontory were.*
> *As well as if a manor of thine own*
> *Or of thine friend's were.*
> *Each man's death diminishes me,*
> *For I am involved in mankind.*
> *Therefore, send not to know*
> *For whom the bell tolls,*
> *It tolls for thee.*

I share that to remind myself as well as you, dear reader, that we are not alone; there is no private truth for me alone or you alone. If I or you find the truth, I am and you are obligated by common decency and the love of neighbor to share that truth. As well, we must constantly remind ourselves that none of us is infallible – all miss the mark and fall short of perfection. Therefore we must not too emphatically promote the truths we find until they have been tested by others, both by those who are pleased to receive them and by those who will resist them with their dying breath.

I am convinced the best way to accomplish this testing is by a collegiate effort to ascertain truth. Here the colleagues are to be not just learned doctors, and certainly not anyone with an axe to grind, but earnest seekers-after-truth who are united not by a particular version of truth, but by a commitment to using a defensible approach to discovering, confirming and reporting the truth they find. The last thing any honest truth seeker should do is to set himself or herself up as an expert, then try

A Match Made In Heaven

to impose his/her version of truth upon the world. God forbid that should ever be true of me or of thee! Amen!

A Match Made In Heaven
CHAPTER IV.

The TruthApp in Action
Extracting Truth from a Mass of Information

Now that you understand that you must know truth if you are going to be free and you have had a look at the process for finding truth, it's time for me to step up to the plate and persuade you that **you can find truth for yourself**. I'm up against a tough pitcher. Have a soda and some popcorn while we learn whether it will be a strikeout or a homerun

None of what we've discussed up to now should have been offensive to either Christian believers or skeptics. We are now about to turn to the Bible as the information source we'll use to illustrate the procedure for establishing truth. It will be best for all, **believers and skeptics alike**, to set aside their biases toward that book and look at it as just a mass of information said to have been compiled over thousands of years.

Its attraction to us is that it is complete; there is no possibility of any new information being added or existing information subtracted. It is a completed work. We will address it as such and not make judgments as to the accuracy of the information contained therein. We will test the "messages" we find there for internal and external consistency, using the criteria established in the previous chapter. Whether the messages are consistent with evidence from outside the Bible is not relevant to our task here, however important that may be in the broader context.

I've set up a companion document – the **RECORD** – for you to refer to as I apply the process. I start that document with the nine steps and I'll record assumptions, hypotheses and conclusions in the Record as they come into play. When we're finished, that document along with this one – the Narrative – will be the project output.

Step 1 is to identify and record the question to be answered or the problem to be solved. This will help maintain focus on the task at hand and make it easier to explain to others exactly what was done.

What I ultimately want to determine is whether scripture teaches that Jesus died on the cross to ransom enslaved mankind from Satan or to accomplish some other purpose. That question has been booted around the outfield for many centuries with no one being able to get a handle on the ball and throw the runner out.

In order to answer that bigger question, we need to know first whether scriptures teach there were people enslaved to Satan at the time of the crucifixion. That is the first question we will explore together in this chapter. If the answer to that is "yes", we'll look at another; Did Jesus give His life to free mankind from slavery or to transfer ownership of Satan's slaves to God? I've recorded those questions in the Record. I will not here address whether Christ died as our substitute since I address that question in Chapter V in an example showing how to test another's understanding of truth.

Step 2 is to determine and summarize in writing the current status of previous and ongoing efforts to answer the question or solve the problem. I've done that too, by copying an existing article you will find in the Record. In some sense, the writer of that article, and all those thinkers who had gone before, appear to have used Origen's heretical "theory" as a straw man in their arguments. And that reminds me to guard myself against creating straw men.

Step 3: Record the **data sources, initial assumptions** and **axioms** that will control the investigation.

The information source we will use is the Bible as we have it today. The Bible says it is the very word of God, and it is said to contain all any person needs to know about who God is,

A Match Made In Heaven

what he is like, who and what man is, and what the relationship between God and man is to be. We will follow the example of the Orthodox Churches and choose the Greek New Testament and the Greek Septuagint Old Testament as our data sources.

We will choose the Septuagint for the same reasons the Orthodox Churches do – the Septuagint was translated before 250 BC, long before the rise of Christianity, by a group of scholars who spoke both Greek and Hebrew. The Masoretic Text, the other available alternative and the source used by Protestants, was compiled over about five centuries beginning in the 5th century AD. The Septuagint predates the first Masoretic Old Testament by over 1000 years, and some writers allege the Masoretic wording was deliberately altered to remove support for the Christian message. That allegation is supported to some extent by discoveries of discrepancies between that text and older copies of the texts found among the Dead Sea Scrolls.

If God is who the Bible says He is, and if He has the powers and knowledge it says He has, we needn't question whether the Bible is what it says it is. The God described in the Bible is perfectly able to cause that book to be written, and perfectly able to preserve it from any attempt to destroy it or change its message. We can be confident we are doing the right thing in choosing the older Greek version; especially since it is much easier for us westerners to understand Greek than Hebrew.

Understand please, our decision to take the Bible as our information source is **an axiom**. We accept it as our data source and will not concern ourselves with questions about its reliability. That important question is outside the bounds of this current investigation.

Our question is, "What does the Bible have to say about these issues?" If we do find a consistent, credible message in words written over thousands of years, that will lend credibility to the claim the Bible makes for itself – that it was written by God for the benefit of mankind. But that is not a question we will consider in this chapter or in this book.

Because we want to understand Bible's message to us, we won't concern ourselves with outside information either. And since translations are easily influenced by the mindset of the translators, we ultimately will rely on the words of the original Greek. Not being skilled in reading Greek, we will use translations for our initial understanding and turn to the Greek for the precise meaning of important words.

I have long used for the basic meaning of Greek words Strong's Exhaustive Concordance of the Bible and Thayer's Greek-English Lexicon of the New Testament. I have found new resources, **E-Sword (www.esword.org)**, a free bible application, and **www.biblelexicon.org,** an online tool, indispensible for this work. I recommend them to you if you are tempted to delve into the Greek yourself.

"These things have been studied to death for a couple of thousand years," you should be thinking about now. "What makes you think you have any chance of coming up with truth that has been overlooked by everyone else?" That's a good question; here's the answer:

The difference is in the approach. I'll take an approach the thinkers of **500** years and more ago couldn't take because the process hadn't been invented yet. We will tackle this body of information just like we would a problem in physics, say, or a crime scene investigation. Follow along and see how this works out. **The Acceptance Criteria we will use in deciding to retain or revise assumptions and hypotheses** taken together, comprise the **axiom** that controls the process. Here are the Acceptance Criteria we will use in all that follows:

1. No accumulation of supporting information can **prove** a hypothesis or assumption, but there must be **some** minimal amount of substantial supporting evidence for the conclusion to

A Match Made In Heaven

be credible. **For this process, the absolute minimum acceptable supporting evidence is determined by God's criterion – there must be at least two (substantial) "witnesses".**

2. It is commonly accepted that a scientific hypothesis (or assumption) must be modified or rejected altogether if even one substantial bit of contradictory information is found to exist. We will be dealing with recorded information, not natural phenomena. Since records can become corrupted and made unreliable, I have adopted for our **Rejection Criterion: an assumption or hypothesis must be rejected if there exist at least two substantial bits of information that could not exist if the assumption or hypothesis were true.**

Here are my initial assumptions:

> *a. There exists, and has existed forever, a spirit being, who created every physical, material thing that now exists, has existed and will exist. He created man in his own image (in some sense) with a specific purpose in mind. He has worked ever since to bring that purpose to fulfillment.*

> *b. He caused to be written, and has preserved for us and those who follow us, a Book, the Bible, containing the information we need to know if we are to understand who He is, what His purpose is for us, and how we are to interact with Him and with His creation, including specifically our fellow man. Every word in that Book has meaning for someone, sometime, someplace, not necessarily for all men in all times and in all places.*

> *c. The message from God to man communicated by the words of the Book is absolutely true and trustworthy, having from the beginning been protected by Him. Included in that message is what we are to know about God – His attributes: omnipotence, omnipresence, perfect knowledge, love, righteousness, justice and truth.*

These assumptions, and all supplementary assumptions, are subject to verification or falsification by evidence contained in the Book.

Step 4: Having identified our data set and listed our axioms and initial assumptions, we are ready to **form a working hypothesis** – a kind of trial theory – that promises to help us discover the answer we are looking for. Once we've recorded that hypothesis so we and others who critique our work can see what we've done, we will begin searching for evidence supporting or contradicting our hypothesis. Finding supporting evidence will encourage us to look further; finding contradictory evidence will mean that we will have to revise our hypothesis or abandon it altogether.

We form our working hypothesis after looking at some of the evidence in the New Testament. Here we see a young man, the son of a carpenter, embarking on a preaching ministry after being baptized by his cousin, John. We're struck by the fact that some of his teaching is in the form of parables.

Why parables? Doesn't he want people to understand what he's telling them? Why go to all that trouble just to leave people in the dark about what he's saying? Jesus said he spoke for the Father (John 14:10). If everything he said came from the Father, and if the Father intended the Bible to communicate a message to us, then he must have had a purpose for speaking in parables. Jesus answers this question in Matthews Gospel:

And the disciples came and said to Him, *"Why do you speak to them in parables?" Jesus answered them, "To you it has been : granted to know the mysteries of the kingdom of heaven, but to them it has not been granted ... Therefore I speak to them in parables; (so that) (while) seeing they do not see, and (while) hearing they do not hear, nor do they understand. "* (Matt 13:10, 13 NASB, edited to show the Greek meanings.)

A Match Made In Heaven

The translation uses "because" instead of "so that"; the Greek word has both meanings. The "seeing" and "hearing" are participles, and properly are translated "while seeing" and "while hearing".

Jesus' answer, as amended, tells us that Jesus taught in parables because God wanted **only His own people** to understand the message of the parable. That would make sense if He knew that rebellious men would distort His message if they understood it. His answer suggests that not all Bible messages are plainly stated, and suggests to us one way God used to preserve the scripture message.

Let's assume that was His purpose. **Let's include that in our working hypothesis – Jesus used parables in part to teach us that not all the Bible's messages are stated plainly and openly, that sometimes the message, though communicated by the words of the text, is not plainly stated.**

Then we recall a conversation Jesus had with a group of Jews "who believed him",

"If you hold to my teaching, you are really my disciples. Then you will know the truth and the truth will set you free"

They answered him, "We are Abraham's descendants and have never been slaves to anyone. How can you say that we shall be set free?"

Jesus replied, "I tell you the truth, everyone who sins is a slave to sin" (John 8:31-34. (NIV)

Here's something interesting. What's this talk about being slaves and being set free? Everyone who sins, he said. Paul tells us all have sinned. (Rom 3:23) Taken together, **those two passages give us another part of our hypothesis – We all are – or have been – slaves – to sin – whatever that means.**

Truth & Freedom

Moving on into Romans, we find a clear statement telling how one can become a slave. *Don't you know that when you offer yourselves to someone to obey him as slaves, you are slaves to the one you obey – whether you are slaves to sin, which leads to death, or to obedience, which leads to righteousness?* (Rom 6:16)

This verse seems to teach us that a person can become a slave simply by agreeing to obey someone.

Now we can write down the initial working hypothesis that will guide us as we begin to look for the message in the scriptures. [Note: What are presented here and in the RECORD are not the actual initial assumptions and hypotheses. Only the final results are presented, there having been far too many mistrials and mistaken assumptions to record in a book of this size.]

Our initial working hypothesis:

a. **The Bible as we have received it, in the plain meaning of the Septuagint and the Greek New Testament, is the information source we'll use to discover God's message. We will not question its accuracy or probability of being true. That is a separate task. Our task is to find the message in the body of information presented to us.**

b. **Using the process described in Chapter 3 will lead us to a credible message from the Bible.**

c. **Jesus used parables in part to teach us that not all the Bible's messages are stated plainly and openly, that sometimes the message communicated by the story is not stated in the words of the story.** (Finding messages not explicitly stated is nothing new in Bible study, we accept many truths that are not explicitly stated, the doctrine of the Trinity being one of them.)

A Match Made In Heaven

    d. **When we encounter material that appears to be a parable, we will look for the message God intends us to find in the parable.**

    e. **We all are or have been slaves to something.** (Jesus said as much; it will pay us to keep that in mind as we progress.)

    f. **A free man can become a slave just by agreeing to obey another, accepting his lordship in exclusion of all others.** We will take the warning in Rom **6:16** to be literally true.

Step 5: Armed with these ideas, this hypothesis, we'll look at the scriptures to try to understand the real situation in which mankind finds it self. We've not yet proved this approach is the proper one. Whether it is will become clear as we see whether it is useful in helping us understand who God is, who we are, and what he intends our relationship to him to be.

Let's now go to the Bible and look at Genesis chapters 2 and 3. Here we find something interesting, two unusual trees and a talking snake. Here are the verses that mention them:

> Gen **2:9** *And out of the ground made the LORD God to grow every tree that is pleasant to the sight, and good for food; the tree of life also in the midst of the garden, and the tree of knowledge of good and evil.*

> Gen **2:16** *And the LORD God commanded the man, saying, Of every tree of the garden thou mayest freely eat:*

> Gen **2:17** *But of the tree of the knowledge of good and evil, thou shalt not eat of it: for in the day that thou eatest thereof thou shalt surely die.*

> Gen **3:1** *Now the serpent was more subtil than any beast of the field which the LORD God had made. And*

he said unto the woman, Yea, hath God said, Ye shall not eat of every tree of the garden?

Gen 3:2 And the woman said unto the serpent, We may eat of the fruit of the trees of the garden:

Gen 3:3 But of the fruit of the tree which is in the midst of the garden, God hath said, Ye shall not eat of it, neither shall ye touch it, lest ye die.

Gen 3:4 And the serpent said unto the woman, Ye shall not surely die:

Gen 3:5 For God doth know that in the day ye eat thereof, then your eyes shall be opened, and ye shall be as gods, knowing good and evil.

Gen 3:6 And when the woman saw that the tree was good for food, and that it was pleasant to the eyes, and a tree to be desired to make one wise, she took of the fruit thereof, and did eat, and gave also unto her husband with her; and he did eat.

Gen 3:7 And the eyes of them both were opened, and they knew that they were naked; and they sewed fig leaves together, and made themselves aprons.

Gen 3:8 And they heard the voice of the LORD God walking in the garden in the cool of the day: and Adam and his wife hid themselves from the presence of the LORD God amongst the trees of the garden.

Gen 3:22 And the LORD God said, Behold, the man is become as one of us, to know good and evil: and now, lest he put forth his hand, and take also of the tree of life, and eat, and live for ever:

A Match Made In Heaven

> Gen 3:23 *Therefore the LORD God sent him forth from the garden of Eden, to till the ground from whence he was taken.*
>
> Gen 3:24 *So he drove out the man; and he placed at the east of the garden of Eden Cherubims, and a flaming sword which turned every way, to keep the way of the tree of life.* (KJV)

(I use the King James Version which was translated in 1608 because the Strong's Numbers I use for word search are keyed to the exact words used in the KJV. You will find modern translations, using other words to communicate the same meaning, much easier to read. Two that I like are the New International Version (NIV) and the New King James Version (NKJV.)

We begin by asking the questions; who, what, when, where, why, and how, taught to journalists. We know the "who" was God; it was He who planted the trees, told Adam what he could eat and what he could not, and who in the end exiled Adam and Eve from the Garden.

What we are looking for is not why God did those things, we assume he does nothing by accident, so that means he had a purpose for planting those trees, etc. and we assume He caused them to be included in His book to teach us something. So the question becomes, "What does He want us to learn from the facts that He placed those trees there and that He told Adam to freely eat the fruit of one but not the other."

One obvious answer to that question is that God wants us to learn from the Tree of Life that He intended Adam, and we assume, his descendants, **to live forever.**

Next question; "What does that tree tell us **about Adam**?" Answer: that Adam was created a mortal man who would die eventually if he did not eat the fruit of the tree of life. Otherwise there would be no purpose for putting the tree in the Garden.

This is a most important finding; **we are**, in this respect at least, **precisely as Adam was when he was created**. Adam was mortal, but was meant to live forever. We are mortal, but God has made a way for us to live forever, just as he made a way for Adam to do so. And we, like Adam, have an opportunity to choose to accept the offer or refuse it.

Now let's look at the Tree of Knowledge. What does God want us to learn about himself from that story, and what does he want us to learn about Adam and ourselves? We know, first, that God created Adam (and Eve) "in His own image." Gen 1:27 *So God created man in his own image, in the image of God created he him; male and female created he them.*

We have seen that "his own image" includes immortality – eternal life. The question now before us is, in what other ways God may have created man in his own image. We have only to look at ourselves and others to know that man does not possess any of the infinite qualities ascribed to God, omnipotence, omniscience, etc.; the finite cannot be infinite.

But there is one quality God may have given to man, and there is reason to believe he did so. That is sovereignty, freedom, free will, the authority and ability to choose how he will act.

God created other intelligent beings, angels at least, and they were created to serve him. He may not have given them authority to choose. They were created to serve God, to obey His commands. We cannot examine here all the reasons God might have wanted such companions, but it seems not unlikely that he created Adam to have the same freedom of choice and action that He, Himself, enjoyed.

I will take as part of His reason for putting the Tree of Knowledge in the Garden was for the express purpose of

A Match Made In Heaven

teaching us that Adam was created a free, sovereign creature, and that we are created such ourselves.

"How does that follow?" you are asking. Here's how: Adam was given the freedom to do or not do what God "suggested" he do. But except for that tree (and the Serpent, of course), he was in a perfect environment, he had no way of exercising his freedom since he could choose only the good. The tree was put there specifically to give Adam an opportunity to choose unwisely.

Adam, not having God's perfect knowledge, did not know how his choice would impact his future. And he'd never encountered a bald-faced liar like the Serpent, so when he saw the tree was beautiful, that the fruit was good to eat, and that Eve hadn't died instantly, he chose to follow the Serpent's instructions rather than God's. We'll see a little later how that turned out.

For now, we will conclude that at least part of the reason God placed the Forbidden Fruit in the Garden was to teach us that Adam was created a free man, and, since we are created in God's image, that he intends all men to be free.

We could spend much more time looking into the messages of the trees, but our task here was to look for this passage being a parable by seeing if there are messages that are not explicitly stated. We found three:

    a. **God intended man to live forever.** Otherwise, God would not have put the Tree of Life in the Garden and told Adam he could eat its fruit whenever he wanted.

    b. **God created Adam a mortal man.** If Adam was immortal, there would be no reason to put the Tree of Life in the Garden and tell Adam he could freely eat its fruit.

c. **God created man to be free.** Otherwise God would not have put the forbidden fruit in the garden. That He gave Adam an **opportunity** not to obey shows that he had the **ability** to **choose** not to obey.

We conclude that God's message is sometimes communicated by parables, a conclusion that supports our working hypothesis.

The idea that Adam was created a mortal flies in the face of the almost universally accepted idea that by disobeying God Adam brought death not just upon himself and all mankind but also upon all living creatures. The basis for that idea is found in this verse, ... *sin entered the world through one man (Adam), and death through sin, and in this way death came to all men, because all sinned* ... (Rom 5:12)

That leads us to look into what the Bible means by "sin", after which we'll look at how death came to all mankind through Adam. Here's what we know about the word translated *sin*:

Strong's Concordance has for the nouns in Romans 5:12, (266) *hamartia*, from (264) *harmatano*, and means, *"offense, sin(ful)"*. The verb – to sin – (264) means properly, to miss the mark (and not share in the prize), i.e., figuratively, to err, especially, morally, to sin, offend, trespass. (The numbers are reference numbers for those words in Strong's Concordance.)

Strong's has for Hebrew words used in the Old Testament and translated "sin",

(817) *guilt; by impl(ication) a fault; also a sin offering: guiltiness, (offering for) sin, trespass (offering).*

(2403) *an offense (sometimes habitual sinfulness), and its penalty, occasion, sacrifice or expiation; also an offender, punishment (of sin), purifying (purification for sin), sin, sinning, sin offering.*

A Match Made In Heaven

The root (**2398**) properly *means to miss, to sin, by inference, to forfeit, lack, expiate, repent, lead astray, condemn (and more)*.

Also used in the Old Testament are (**7686**) *to stray, to mistake*; (**5771**) *perversity, i.e., evil;* (**819** feminine of **817**) *guiltiness, a fault, the presentation of a sin offering.*

Vines Complete Expository Dictionary of Old and New Testament Words, copyright **1996**, page **234** states; *The Septuagint translates the group of words with the verb hamartano and derived nouns 540 times. They occur 265 times in the New Testament. ... The New Testament development is that Christ, "having made one sacrifice for sins for all time sat down at the right hand of God ...For by one offering he has perfected for all time those who are being sanctified."*

We learn from all this

1) That the Greek word, *hamartia,* has the same root meaning as the Hebrew – *to miss* (the mark).

2) The flavor is along the lines of a mistake or miscalculation that produces an unintended and undesired result, rather than deliberate disobedience or rebellion.

3) Most importantly, the Hebrew (**817**) (**2403**) can *mean the offense, its penalty, or the sacrifice or expiation for the offence.* It is reasonable to think the Hebrew writers of the New Testament carried all those meanings over into the Greek of the New Testament and **we will assume they did so.**

Before going further, let's see if God actually commanded Adam not to eat the fruit of the tree, or if another word is used. If Adam was created a free person, then we must decide what grounds God had for commanding him to do something. One only commands those who are subordinate to him, that is, his slaves, one of inferior rank, and the like. Genesis 2:16, 17 read:

Gen 2:16 *And the LORD God **commanded** the man, saying, Of every tree of the garden thou mayest freely eat:*

Gen 2:17 *But of the tree of the knowledge of good and evil, thou shalt not eat of it: for in the day that thou eatest thereof thou shalt surely die.* (KJV)

The Hebrew for "command" has the meaning. *enjoin*. Enjoin means, "to direct or impose by command or with urgent admonition." (Webster's Ninth New Collegiate Dictionary) The Greek word (LXX) *eneteilato*, (enjoined) also is translated "commanded"; Its tense is aorist – expressing action at an unspecified (past) time; its voice is middle – the action reflects back onto the speaker, or the speaker has a personal interest in the commanded ones response; its mood is indicative – a simple statement about something.

The middle voice is interesting; it cannot have been used to show God was commanding or warning Himself, so it must have meant He had a personal interest in Adam's obedience. In modern American English, the sentence might read, *And the Lord God admonished the man, saying, it will not please me if you eat the fruit of the tree of knowledge of good and evil...*

He certainly had a personal interest in Adam's response if, as is surely true, He knew Adam's disobedience would lead to His Only Begotten being tortured to death on a cross.

That God was warning Adam, admonishing him, not commanding him, is consistent with Adam having been created a free man.

We learn in the Genesis passage that the Serpent convinced Adam and Eve to trust him instead of God by implying that God had lied to them. Adam, faced with conflicting

A Match Made In Heaven

information and the evidence of his eyes – we imagine Eve standing there grinning at him, with juice running down her chin, obviously alive – trusted what the Serpent (that is, Satan) told him and began to do what he told him to do, that is, what God warned him he should not do.

Hamartia, in the sense of mistake or miscalculation, fits perfectly here. Adam was not God's slave so was free to do what seemed right to him. Failing to take advice is not a transgression of moral law, and it's much different from disobeying a clear order from one in authority.

Romans 6:16 leads us to believe that by choosing to listen to and act upon what the Serpent said instead of heeding God's warning, Adam – a free man – accepted Satan's lordship, and in so doing became his slave.

Notice that we haven't proved this. It's still just an idea we're testing against the scriptures. If it helps us understand the things we need to know, and if nothing in scriptures shows it can't be true, then we can accept it as a valid description of what God wants us to learn from this passage.

Now let's look at what it means to be a slave, and how Adam's foolish choice affected the entire race. We need not go outside the Bible for information about slavery – the Bible is self-contained.

We learn from Lev 25:35-55 that a slave is property, a form of livestock that can be bought, sold, and even willed as an inheritance to ones children. We learn in Exodus 21:2-4 that the children of a slave are themselves slaves and property of the slave's owner, just as a calf is the property of the cow's owner. That being true, it follows that Adam's slavery was passed on to his children and their children, potentially forever.

We know also, though I've not found it stated in the Bible, that a slave must obey his (or her) master. He has no choice. If he doesn't, the master has the right to punish him in any way he thinks appropriate, including killing him if he thinks that's in his own interest.

Because a slave must obey his master, he cannot really own property himself. The master can order him to give the property to him, and the slave must obey or the property will be taken from him and the slave punished. The slave has no thing of value with which to purchase his freedom from the master – the master already owns every thing the slave has, even his wife and children.

The slave cannot work off his purchase price – his labor already belongs to his master. A slave has no way of freeing himself; if he is to be free, his master must set him free. The fact that historically slaves have sometimes purchased their freedom cannot be used to challenge these statements; those slaves had benevolent masters who allowed their slaves to accumulate wealth and purchase their freedom.

Another person cannot justly free a slave forcefully, or by stealth or deceit take him from his master. The slave legally belongs to the master and the master is justified in using any means at his disposal to return the slave to his possession and his service.

Since a slave has no way of freeing himself, he will remain a slave for life unless someone can convince his master to free him. That fact sheds light on God's putting Adam and Eve out of the Garden where they'd not be able to eat the fruit of the Tree of Life. Think about Adam's situation if he had eaten that fruit – he and all his descendants would have been Satan's slaves for eternity.

God's putting Adam and Eve out of the Garden was an act of love – not punishment – just as His giving them clothing was a loving act.

A Match Made In Heaven

Does the fact that Adam was enslaved necessarily mean all mankind is too? Genesis doesn't specifically say God created only Adam and Eve. Some think there must have been others. They wonder where Cain found his wife, and where Adam's sons and daughters found their mates.

God settles that question in the flood story and the genealogies preceding it. Only Noah – descended from Adam and therefore a slave to Satan – and his sons and the four wives, survived the flood. It doesn't matter that God may have created others in the beginning. Whether he did or didn't, the Bible story clearly is the story of Adam and his male descendants and no one else.

And that's the last word on the question of how Adam affected the entire race – his foolishness ended up enslaving all mankind. And his being put out of the Garden put the tree of life forever out of reach of Adam and his progeny. In this sense, and in this sense only, he brought death to all mankind.

If God had been willing to let his adversary simply steal his greatest creation (in our obviously biased opinion) from him, we'd have no Bible and we'd not be doing this study. God put in place (or already had in place) a plan for recovering mankind from the one who'd stolen it from him through lies and deceit. God is the Lawgiver, and cannot righteously and justly ignore those laws to another's loss. He could not justly take Satan's legally acquired slaves from him.

Before we further explore God's plan, let's pause to put a few more pieces of the message in place. Here we will explore the laws that God put in place to govern his creation. We can identify three sets of laws: (I did "invent" this idea, but was far from the first to do so. The idea goes back as least as far as Thomas Aquinas, and perhaps back to the ancient Greek philosophers.)

First, the physical laws – laws that govern interactions among material things. These are not discussed in the scriptures, but we know from scientific discoveries of at least the past four centuries that such laws exist and almost certainly have existed from the beginning.

Second, the social laws – laws that govern interactions among rational beings. We assume – **another assumption** – that **the Ten Commandments are a brief subset of the Social Law.**

We assume further **that Exodus through Deuteronomy provide further details of those laws**, and **the cursing and blessing of Deuteronomy 27 & 28 apply to all mankind**, whether they are aware of the laws or not, **just as do the physical laws**.

Some might interpret Hebrews 7:18, 19 as teaching the Social Laws were abolished because of their inability to save: *For, on the one hand, there is a setting aside of a former commandment because of its weakness and uselessness, (for the Law made nothing perfect), and on the other hand there is a bringing in of a better hope, through which we draw near to God.* (NASB)

A quick look at the Greek and the context shows this is not what is taught there. The word translated "commandment" is not *nomos*, the word translated everywhere as "Law", but another word also meaning commandment. The context clearly shows that the ceremonial law, with its sacrifices and priesthood, was annulled when God replaced the Aaronite priesthood with a new High Priest from the tribe of David. External supporting evidence that this is so is the fact that God's Chosen People have lived without the temple, and thus the sacrifices and the priesthood for nearly 2000 years.

Third, the ceremonial laws – laws put in place to let obedient Israelites who unknowingly or unintentionally transgress, escape the curse God pronounced on those who violate any of the social laws. The ceremonial laws are enumerated primarily in Leviticus.

A Match Made In Heaven

We touched on some of the social laws above; now we want to expand the set a little. Here we are interested in the social laws governing interactions between men and their women, and **we will assume**, between masters and their slaves.

> Num **30:1** *And Moses spake unto the heads of the tribes concerning the children of Israel, saying, This is the thing which the LORD hath commanded.*
>
> Num **30:2** *If a man vow a vow unto the LORD, or swear an oath to bind his soul with a bond; he shall not break his word, he shall do according to all that proceedeth out of his mouth.*
>
> Num **30:3** *If a woman also vow a vow unto the LORD, and bind herself by a bond, being in her father's house in her youth;*
>
> Num **30:4** *And her father hear her vow, and her bond wherewith she hath bound her soul, and her father shall hold his peace at her: then all her vows shall stand, and every bond wherewith she hath bound her soul shall stand.*
>
> Num **30:5** *But if her father disallow her in the day that he heareth; not any of her vows, or of her bonds wherewith she hath bound her soul, shall stand: and the LORD shall forgive her, because her father disallowed her.*
>
> Num **30:6** *And if she had at all an husband, when she vowed, or uttered ought out of her lips, wherewith she bound her soul;*
>
> Num **30:7** *And her husband heard it, and held his peace at her in the day that he heard it: then her vows shall stand, and her bonds wherewith she bound her soul shall stand.*

Num 30:8 *But if her husband disallowed her on the day that he heard it; then he shall make her vow which she vowed, and that which she uttered with her lips, wherewith she bound her soul, of none effect: and the LORD shall forgive her.*

Num 30:9 *But every vow of a widow, and of her that is divorced, wherewith they have bound their souls, shall stand against her.*

Num 30:10 *And if she vowed in her husband's house, or bound her soul by a bond with an oath;*

Num 30:11 *And her husband heard it, and held his peace at her, and disallowed her not: then all her vows shall stand, and every bond wherewith she bound her soul shall stand.*

Num 30:12 *But if her husband hath utterly made them void on the day he heard them; then whatsoever proceeded out of her lips concerning her vows, or concerning the bond of her soul, shall not stand: her husband hath made them void; and the LORD shall forgive her.*

Num 30:13 *Every vow, and every binding oath to afflict the soul, her husband may establish it, or her husband may make it void.*

Num 30:14 *But if her husband altogether hold his peace at her from day to day; then he establisheth all her vows, or all her bonds, which are upon her: he confirmeth them, because he held his peace at her in the day that he heard them.*

Num 30:15 *But if he shall any ways make them void after that he hath heard them; then he shall bear her iniquity.*

A Match Made In Heaven

> Num 30:16 *These are the statutes, which the LORD commanded Moses, between a man and his wife, between the father and his daughter, being yet in her youth in her father's house.*

God communicated these rules to Israel long after Abraham arrived on the scene, but they are important to understanding a crucial part of the story. We will assume – **another assumption**

These rules have from the beginning been part of God's Social Law, and they apply not just to a man and his wife or daughter, but to all situations where one person is subservient to another.

Here we see a man, still a slave to God as we will see, given certain freedoms and responsibilities under the law, and a wife or unmarried daughter not given that freedom. That is, the woman is for practical purposes a slave of the man, perhaps even so far as being considered his property. But a woman who has been set free from these rules either by being sent away by her husband or by her husband's death, has the same freedom and responsibilities a man has; she is responsible for the choices she makes. (That likely is her status today if her husband or father has abdicated his God given responsibility to protect his wife or daughter as husbands and fathers too often do in this country in these times.)

Biblically, an unmarried daughter or a wife does not have a man's freedom and responsibility; she depends on her father or her husband to determine what she may do. Note too, that the husband must forbid the woman to act as she plans "on the day that he hears it." If he doesn't, the woman is free – in fact, is obligated – to act. We assume – not a new assumption – the same applies to masters and slaves – if the master does not forbid a slave to act, on the day he hears it, then the slave is free to do what he has told his master he intends to do.

We will see how important this assumption is for understanding the Bible Message as we progress.

God advanced His plan to rescue mankind when he contacted Abram – later called Abraham – and still a slave of Satan – and told him to go to a land he promised to give him and his descendants. That contact later led to Abraham's grandson, Jacob – now called Israel – moving his family to Egypt to escape a region-wide famine. There they were tasked with tending Pharaoh's livestock and were given the land of Goshen to live in.

God moved his plan forward another step some 430 years later when he worked through Moses to induce the then Pharaoh to free the Israelites to *"... go serve the Lord as ye have said."* (Exodus **12:31** KJV) By that time the people had greatly increased in number and power and the Egyptians had begun to fear them, so they enslaved them, forcing them to construct several cities for them. God assigned Moses the task of freeing the people from this slavery.

Easily overlooked in the stories telling how Aaron and Moses carried out God's plan to free Israel, is a puzzling but important couple of verses. God speaking to Moses, *Then you shall say to Pharaoh, thus says the Lord: Israel is My son, My firstborn. So I say to you, let My son go that he may serve Me. But if you refuse to let him go, indeed, I will kill your son, your firstborn.* (Exodus **4:22, 23** NKJV)

We ask ourselves how God can truthfully say, *"Israel is my son, my firstborn."* We know God never lies and that the Bible was given to instruct us, so what can it mean to call Israel (Jacob) God's firstborn son?

Here is what we know:

1.   Israel/Jacob was the son of Isaac, the son of Abraham.

A Match Made In Heaven

2. Thayer has for son G5207 – **huios** – **i.** prop(erly) **a.** *rarely of the young of animals ... generally of the offspring of men, and in the restricted sense, male issue (one begotten by a father and born of a mother)* **ii.** *... according to the Hebrew mode of speech, with the genitive of a person, refers to anyone who depends on another or is his follower.* "My" in the Septuagint is genitive singular.

3. A slave is dependent upon his master for everything.

4. God could truthfully call Jacob his (figurative) son if Isaac were His slave. (Remember that genitive "my".)

5. Isaac would have been born God's slave if Abraham was His slave. But in that case, wouldn't God have called Isaac his firstborn?

The question, then, is how Abraham, Satan's slave, could have a son, Isaac, who was God's slave. I suggest the following sequence of actions:

> **a.** Abraham told Satan, or his representative, that he intended to take Isaac to Mount Moriah and there sacrifice him to the Lord.
>
> **b.** Satan, or his representative, did not "in the day that he heard it", tell Abraham he was forbidden to sacrifice Isaac.
>
> **c.** Abraham carried out God's instructions, believing as we are told in Hebrews, that God would restore Isaac to life.
>
> **d.** God surprised everyone by accepting Isaac as a living sacrifice, accepting him as His slave.

Isaac had two sons, the elder of which sold his birthright to the younger for a mess of pottage. The second-born son in this way acquired the rights of the firstborn and thus became (figuratively) God's firstborn.

Based on the above, we conclude:

Jacob and all his family, including also his slaves, were God's slaves from a time long before the Exodus took place. God was dealing with His Own People throughout the 40 years of wandering in the desert and He has been throughout all history since.

I advance this idea with some trepidation – it is not completely clear that Ex 4:22, 23 should be understood that way. However, until a better explanation of those verses is brought forth, I will stick with this one. As we will see in a bit, it is certainly clear that the Israelites were God's people – His slaves – when He rescued them from their Egyptian bondage.

Up till now we have been concerned with what happened to Adam's seed through the first five books of the Bible. We have seen:

a. **Adam's foolish choice enslaved himself, Eve and all their descendants to Satan**

b. **God, in putting the First Couple out of the Garden, was acting in love, not wrath as is so often preached and taught.**

c. **Because God freely chose not to disobey the laws He created to govern interactions between rational beings, He waited a long, long time before acting to free His prized creation from slavery.**

d. **By giving Isaac to God as a living sacrifice, Abraham, still a slave to Satan, provided the seed for a race owing its allegiance to God.**

A Match Made In Heaven

    e. That race, at the time of the Exodus and through history since was and remains God's property, His personal possession, His people, and the apple of His eye.

We have one more piece to add to this portion of God's message, an episode near the end of Joshua's life. He had led the invasion of the Promised Land, had obeyed Moses' command to assemble the people on Mounts Ebal and Gerizim and had read to them the Law with its blessing and cursing. Then he had led the people as they rid the land of most of its inhabitants and supervised the allotting of land to the tribes. Now Joshua was old and the land was at peace. He called the tribes and the people together, and they assembled themselves before God.

Joshua, speaking for the Lord, recounted all He had done for them from the Exodus through the conquest of the land and the peace they now enjoyed. Then he said to the people:

> Jos 24:14 *Now therefore fear the LORD, and serve him in sincerity and in truth: and put away the gods which your fathers served on the other side of the flood, and in Egypt; and serve ye the LORD.*

> Jos 24:15 *And if it seem evil unto you to serve the LORD, choose you this day whom ye will serve; whether the gods which your fathers served that were on the other side of the flood, or the gods of the Amorites, in whose land ye dwell: but as for me and my house, we will serve the LORD.*

> Jos 24:16 *And the people answered and said, God forbid that we should forsake the LORD, to serve other gods;*

> Jos 24:17 *For the LORD our God, he it is that brought us up and our fathers out of the land of Egypt, from the house of bondage, and which did those great signs in*

our sight, and preserved us in all the way wherein we went, and among all the people through whom we passed

Jos 24:*19* And Joshua said unto the people, Ye cannot serve the LORD: for he is an holy God; he is a jealous God; he will not forgive your transgressions nor your sins.

Jos 24:20 If ye forsake the LORD, and serve strange gods, then he will turn and do you hurt, and consume you, after that he hath done you good.

Jos 24:21 And the people said unto Joshua, Nay; but we will serve the LORD.

Jos 24:22 And Joshua said unto the people, Ye are witnesses against yourselves that ye have chosen you the LORD, to serve him. And they said, We are witnesses.

Jos 24:23 Now, therefore put away, said he, the strange gods which are among you, and incline your heart unto the LORD God of Israel.

Jos 24:24 And the people said unto Joshua, The LORD our God will we serve, and his voice will we obey.

Jos 24:25 So Joshua made a covenant with the people that day, and set them a statute and an ordinance in Shechem.

Jos 24:26 And Joshua wrote these words in the book of the law of God, and took a great stone, and set it up there under an oak, that was by the sanctuary of the LORD.

Jos 24:27 And Joshua said unto all the people, Behold, this stone shall be a witness unto us; for it hath heard all the words of the LORD which he spake unto us; it shall

A Match Made In Heaven

be therefore a witness unto you, lest ye deny your God. (KJV)

Here we see the Lord God offering his slaves an opportunity to stop serving Him and turn their allegiance to other gods. That they were at that time God's slaves is shown by **24:16**, *God forbid that we should forsake the LORD, to serve other gods.* They were serving the Lord at that time. God gave them an opportunity to change masters and all Israel declined the offer, cementing their relationship with God for the ages to come.

We'll not further follow this trail through the Old Testament, having developed ample evidence to show that Adam's foolish choice enslaved all mankind to Satan, and that God, with the cooperation of Abraham rescued a portion of mankind from that slavery. Notice, too, that by making them His slaves, He assured that Satan could not enslave them again – they belonged to God, and were not free to choose whom they would serve. God would not let these people be stolen from Him.

We have looked at only **6** of the **39** books in the Protestant version of the Old Testament – 14 additional books are included in the Greek Orthodox Bible. Until all those scriptures are searched for incompatible evidence, we can't be completely confident that this is a credible message. Probably that will take several years to work out. In the meantime, we can be confident in believing it meets the credibility requirements of our criteria for acceptance.

Step 6 We found it unnecessary to further amend the working hypothesis, axioms and assumptions because they lead to an internally consistent understanding of the scriptures

Step 7. We now look at the New Testament to see if there is evidence of slaves of Satan living in Jesus' time.

Truth & Freedom

Our hypothesis suggests there must have been and Scripture confirms it.

The Greek New Testament uses 7 words, – 3 verbs and 4 nouns – to describe the process of freeing the enslaved. The verbs are: **exagorazo** meaning to buy up, to ransom; **lutroo**, meaning to redeem, liberate by payment of ransom; and **agorazo**, meaning to go to market, to purchase.

The nouns are: **antilutron,** meaning a redemption price, what is given in exchange for another as the price of his redemption or ransom, **apolutrosis,** meaning, a ransom in full, a redemption obtained by paying the price; **lutron,** meaning a price for redeeming, ransom; **lutrosis**, meaning a ransoming, deliverance.

Please note, all of the words involving *lutron* and its derivatives are commonly used to describe the freeing of persons who have freely sold themselves into slavery, or who were taken by force, as in a battle, and were held by their captors with the expectation of being paid for setting them free or returning them to their master.

Nineteen verses in the New Testament describe Christ's redeeming or ransoming of mankind. (One of those verses is an exact copy of another.) The verses and Greek words used are:

> **antilutron**: 1 Tim 2:6
>
> **apolutrosis**: Lk 21:28; Rom 3:24, 8:23; 1Cor 1:30; Eph 1:7, 1:14, 4:30; Col 1:14; Heb 9:15, 11:35
>
> **lutron**: Mat 20:28; Mk 10:45 (The verses are identical in the Greek.)
>
> **lutroo**: Lk 24:21; Tit 2:14; 1 Pet 1:18
>
> **lutrosis**: Lk 1:68, 2:38; Heb 9:12

A Match Made In Heaven

Ten verses speak of purchasing, being purchased:

agarazo: 1 Cor 6:20, 7:23; 2 Pet 2:1; Rev 5:9, 14:3,4

exagorazo: Gal 3:13, 4:5; Eph 5:16; Col 4:5

With two exceptions, each of these verses teaches ransom, or purchase, of slaves. The exceptions are Rev 14:3, 4, which speak of the 144,000 redeemed in the end times. There is no conflict between "purchase" in some contexts and "ransom" in others; ransom involves the exchange of something of value for something valued, a purchase.

None of these verses specifically says that Christ redeemed men from Satan, but all do speak of redeeming slaves, and scripture provides no other possible slave master. It appears that Origen in teaching that Christ's self sacrifice redeemed mankind from slavery was correct; he erred in concocting a story to explain how that was done.

Conclusion: There were slaves of Satan existing at the time of Jesus' self sacrifice.

We've found solid evidence that there were slaves, presumably Satan's slaves, existing in Jesus' time, thus answering our first question. Now let's look at the second question: "Did Jesus give His life to free mankind from slavery or to transfer ownership of Satan's slaves to God?" Here are the verses that teach that Christ's sacrifice transferred ownership to God:

> *Or do you not know that your body is a temple of the Holy Spirit who is in you, whom you have from God, and that* **you are not your own? For you have been bought with a price:** *therefore glorify God in your body* 1 Cor 6:19,20.
>
> *For he who was called in the Lord while a slave is the Lord's freedman; likewise he who was called while free,*

Truth & Freedom

is Chris's slave. **You were bought with a price; do not become slaves of men.** 1 Cor 7:22,23

... who gave Himself for us to redeem us from every lawless deed, and to purify **for Himself a people for His own possession,** *zealous for good deeds.* Tit 2:14

But false prophets also arose among the people, just as there will also be false teachers among you, who will secretly introduce destructive heresies, even denying **the Master who bought them,** *bringing swift destruction upon themselves.* 2 Pet 2:1

And they sang a new song, saying, "Worthy are You to take the book and to break its seals; for You were slain, and **purchased for God with Your blood men from every tribe and tongue and people and nation."** Rev 5:9

These five verses do not in themselves satisfy the criterion we adopted for establishing credibility, but they do satisfy God's minimum criterion that there be at least two (substantial) witnesses. Therefore we can conclude with confidence that Christ's self-sacrifice transferred ownership of Satan's slaves to God. I know of no evidence that God subsequently set all mankind free. Therefore we must conclude that, unless we have accepted God's offer to set us free, we remain His slaves, His property.

We've seen Jesus did die to transfer ownership of Satan's slaves to God. We have seen no evidence suggesting Jesus died instead to free Satan's slaves. So the answer to the second question is Jesus did die to transfer ownership of Satan's slaves to God, His death did not set mankind free from slavery.

Conclusion: Jesus died not to set men free, but to transfer ownership from Satan to God.

A Match Made In Heaven

Notice that transferring ownership was a necessary precondition for setting former slaves free; even God cannot justly interfere between a legally acquired slave and his master. Whether setting men free was in God's mind when He planned this event is a question beyond the scope of the task we set ourselves in the beginning. Therefore, we must conclude "redemption" and "salvation" (setting free) are separate events, the first being a necessary precursor to the second.

One more thought before concluding this study: Israelites living in Jesus' time already belonged to God; they did not need a redeemer. In rejecting Christ, they forfeited the other benefits of His self-sacrifice. By refusing to accept Jesus as their Messiah, they reject the One who can set them free. And by rejecting Jesus as God's new High Priest, and in abandoning the no longer operative Ceremonial Law, they forfeited their only way of removing the curse imposed on violators of the Social Law.

These sons of Israel, the apple of God's eye, deceived by leaders unwilling to bow the neck to a new reality, are cursed to live like slaves of Satan though no Israelite has been his slave for most of 4000 years. They are, of all peoples of the earth, the most to be pitied.

Step 8. This Chapter provides the required report in an appropriate medium.

Step 9: In completing this narrative and the Record – attached as Appendix III., we have completed this step and this investigation.

This chapter is an example showing how to use the 9-step process of chapter III to develop credible and defendable conclusions from a body of information. Whether the conclusions reached are defendable against those who prefer not to accept them will be determined by the nature and quality of the attacks brought against them. If our tools are worthy of the battle, they will be up to the defense; if not, they are less than I believe them to be, and they will in the end go to the scrapheap, the ultimate destination of everything worthless.

So there you have it. I trust you have enjoyed reading and working through this chapter and will soon apply its method in discovering truth for yourself!

A Match Made In Heaven
CHAPTER V.

The LieBot In Action

Testing the Credibility of a Message

Now that we know why Jesus sacrificed himself, let's have a look at the two theories of atonement that guide the teaching and practice of nearly all Christians. If we find either of those widely held theories is not believable, that will distress many who believe their version of the theory is Christianity's true message. I hope I can ease any such anxiety by reminding them of some New Testament truths not impacted by either theory of atonement and believed by all Christians. (The following are from NASB, 1995 edition)

First, All who call upon the name of Jesus will be saved:

...so that whoever believes will in Him have eternal life; **John 3:15**;

...but these have been written so that you may believe that Jesus is the Christ, the Son of God; and that believing you may have life in His name, **John 20:31**;

And it shall be that whoever calls on the name of the Lord will be saved **Acts 2:21**;

...for Whoever will call on the name of the Lord will be saved, **Rom 10:13**.

These verses teach us that anyone who believes on the name of Jesus Christ can be sure he will be saved.

Second, Believers will be remade in the image of Jesus.

Just as we have borne the image of the earthy, we will also bear the image of the heavenly. **1 Cor 15:49**;

But we all, with unveiled face, beholding as in a mirror the glory of the Lord, are being transformed into the same image from glory to glory, just as from the Lord, the Spirit. **2 Cor 3:18**;

...in reference to your former manner of life, you lay aside the old self, which is being corrupted in accordance with the lusts of deceit and that you be renewed in the spirit of your mind, and put on the new self, which in the likeness of God has been created in righteousness and holiness of the truth. **Eph 4:22-24**;

...who will transform the body of our humble state into conformity with the body of His glory, **Phil 3:21**;

Do not lie to one another, since you laid aside the old self with its evil practices, and have put on the new self who is being renewed to a true knowledge according to the image of the One who created him, **Col 3:9,10**;

...since Christ also suffered for you, leaving you an example for you to follow in His steps. **1 Pet 2:21**.

Clearly, God approves of anyone who is being transformed into the likeness of His Son, no matter how that is being done.

Third, *Christians are to "love the Lord God with all their mind, will and strength, and their neighbors as themselves,"* **Mk 12:30,31.**

Fourth, Christians are to avoid sinful behavior, Gal 5:19-21

Fifth, Christians are to serve God, Rom 12:11, Col 3:24.

Sixth, Christians are to obey those God gives authority over them, Rom 13.

It is true that God acknowledges and rewards anyone turning to Him, but I don't want you to think it doesn't make any

A Match Made In Heaven

difference what you believe so long as you believe some of God's truths. One problem with believing what is not true, is that believing it robs you of two blessings, the blessing God has for those who obey Him, and the ability to choose to do what is in your best interest to do. That's another way of saying, untruths make slaves and truth sets men free.

Some who fully understand that fact, pile on non-scriptural requirements until they control every important decision their followers make, from how and where they spend their time to how and where they spend their money. In extreme cases, they even control how they die – I'm thinking of the Jim Jones Kool-Aid drinkers and the Branch Dravidians burned alive by U.S. Government agents. *It was for freedom that Christ set us free; therefore keep standing firm and do not be subject again to a yoke of slavery.* Gal 5:1. This is a verse well taken to heart.

Now let's turn to this Chapter's task for me, showing how you can know whether a message is credible or not credible. You will recall that a credible message must be consistent internally – which means there are no flaws in logic or reasoning, and it must be consistent externally – there exists substantial supporting evidence and no incompatible external evidence has been found. I will show you in what follows that what we concluded in Chapter IV. is incompatible with both the Substitution and the Satisfaction theories of atonement.

The ransom theory was one of several views of atonement advanced during the first thousand years of Christian history. Though the Church did not accept any theory about how it was accomplished, the entire Christian Church did accept without question for over 1000 years that Jesus' death in some way redeemed (i.e. ransomed) mankind from slavery to Satan

St. Anselm, the 11th century Archbishop of Canterbury, argued against that view, saying that Satan, being himself a rebel and outlaw, could never have a just claim on humans. He went on to construct the **Satisfaction Theory of Atonement;** he assumed it was not slavery that separates man from God but it's that man's sin dishonors God, and that causes the separation. Having made that assumption, he invented a reason for Jesus sacrificing himself.

Anselm's solution – his invention – was that any deviation from God's perfect will for man dishonors God, no matter whether accidental or deliberate. Because God's honor has been impugned, God must have **satisfaction** for the insult. Only the death of a completely sinless and infinitely worthy man could provide that satisfaction.

While this seems arbitrary and capricious to us, the following excerpt from a Wikipedia article (reformatted and Americanized for our use) explains how Anselm came to develop the theory in the way he did.

[**Begin Quote**]

> *In order to better understand the historical situation in which Anselm developed his argument one must recall that medieval common law developed out of Germanic tribal law, in which one finds the principle of the **werguid**, i.e., the value which a man's life had, determined by his social standing within a tribal community. Thus if a man killed a slave, he owed the owner of the slave the amount of money he had paid for the slave or would have to pay to buy another slave of equal worth.*
>
> *If a man killed another free man he forfeited his own life, unless the slain man's family or tribe agreed to accept some amount of money or goods equal to the value of the slain free man's life within his own tribal group. Again, a man's honor is conceived of in terms of his social standing within his own tribal group. Thus, a slave has no honor since he is owned by another, but a free man's social standing is equal to that of another free*

A Match Made In Heaven

man within his tribal group, but is subordinate to that of his tribal king.

A free man will therefore defend his own honor with his life, or forfeit it (i.e., his social standing within his tribal group) and any affront to his honor by another free man must be repaid by the other man's forfeiting of his own life. Hence the custom of fighting duels. One who committed an affront to another man's honor or would not defend his own affronted honor would be regarded as a coward and suffer outlawry, i.e., he would lose his own social value and standing within his trib(e) and anyone could kill him without fear of retaliation from the man's tribal group.

Thus, since God is infinite, his honor is infinite and any affront to his honor requires from humanity an infinite satisfaction. Furthermore, as humanity's Creator, God is humanity's Master and humanity has nothing of its own with (which) to compensate for this affront to his honor. God, nevertheless, must require something of equal value to his divine honor, otherwise God would forfeit his own essential dignity as God.

Anselm resolves the dilemma thus created by maintaining that since Christ is both God and man he can act as humanity's champion, (i.e., as a man he is a member of humanity—again, conceived of in tribal terms. i.e., Christ is member of the human tribe, with all the standing and social responsibilities inherent in such membership) he can pay the infinite werguid the humanity owes the slighted divine honor, for while the life he forfeits to pay this werguid on humanity's behalf is a human life, it is the human life of his divine person thus has the infinite value proper to his divine person. (At) the same time, Christ is also God and thus his divine person and his human life, as the human life of his divine person, has infinite value.

Thus by offering his human life (with its nevertheless infinite value as the human life of his divine person) as the **werguid** *humanity owes his divine Master for humanity's affront to his divine honor as God. At the same time, Christ as God acts as the champion of the infinite dignity of his own divine honor as God and Master of humanity by accepting as God the infinite value of the werguid of his own human life as the human life of his own divine person as the proper and only sufficient* **werguid** *due to his own divine honor.*

One might thus interpret Anselm's understanding of the Cross in terms of duel fought between Christ's identification with humanity as a man and his divine honor as God in which the claims of both his human and divine natures are met, vindicated and thus reconciled. **[End of Quote] The entire article is available at** http://en.wikipedia.org/wiki/Penal_substitution.

This information shows us that Anselm's theory makes perfect sense if God is a German Tribal Chief, constrained by German tribal law. Of course He is not, and Anselm commits the double error of ignoring the scriptural teachings on Ransom, and imagining God can be insulted by what man does. These errors led him to the conclusion that God must be vindicated by the death of those who insult Him. His double error led Anselm to develop what is clearly not believable, i.e., it is incredible.

From the same article – from which you can learn much by reading – we learn how John Calvin modified Anselm's Satisfaction Theory to form the Penal Substitution Theory.

Calvin appropriated Anselm's ideas but changed the terminology to that of the criminal law with which he was familiar - he was trained as a lawyer - reinterpreted

A Match Made In Heaven

in the light of Biblical teaching on the law. Man is guilty before God's judgment and the only appropriate punishment is eternal death. The Son of God has become man and has stood in man's place to bear the immeasurable weight of wrath; the curse, and the condemnation of a righteous God. He was "made a substitute and a surety in the place of transgressors and even submitted as a criminal, to sustain and suffer all the punishment which would have been inflicted on them."

The work of the Reformers, including Zwingli and Philip Melanchthon, was hugely influential. It took away from religion the requirement of works, whether corporal or spiritual, of the need for penances, belief in purgatory, indeed the whole medieval penitential system; and it did so by emphasizing the finality of Christ's work. **[End of Quote]**

Calvin followed Anselm in ignoring scripture's teaching on the ransom and in assuming God's Laws are like Man's laws, for him the French penal system. As with Anselm, we will find his flawed foundation cannot support the weight of his conclusions.

We understand where both Anselm and Calvin went wrong, but that is irrelevant to the task before us. We are here to test whether Calvin's Substitution Theory is credible, that is, if it is supported by substantial evidence. We showed in Chapter IV that there is substantial evidence that could not exist if the Penal Substitution Theory is true. Here we will test whether there is substantial evidence supporting Calvin's incompatible theory. If we find Calvin's theory to be credible, then we are faced with two credible, but incompatible theories. In such cases, we must decide which we will believe by applying the method described in chapter III.

Following is a brief summary of the Substitution Theory, constructed of statements by advocates of the theory. I couldn't find a complete statement so constructed this one. I certainly do not want to mislead anyone by using the Straw Man fallacy. If I've included anything that is not part of the theory, or omitted something that is, please let me know so I can correct the error.

> *Any sin, any transgression, any falling short of God's perfect will for us makes us guilty. It's not only our own actions that condemn us; God imputes to each of Adam's descendants Adam's sin or the guilt thereof. Because of who and what He is, God cannot associate with those guilty of sin; He has ordained that all sin is punishable by death.*
>
> *God loves humans and wants to be reconciled with them. That is not possible as long as they remain guilty of sin. Only the blood sacrifice of a perfectly innocent man can remove the guilt and atone for mankind's sins. Jesus, being God's true Son, and guiltless because he was sinless, was the acceptable sacrifice that could atone for our sin, allowing God to forgive us and cleanse us so that we could associate with Him.*
>
> *Jesus willingly allowed himself to be sacrificed in our place, taking our guilt upon himself. God imputed to this innocent man all the sins of the world and allowed him **to carry away** the sins of the whole world, the way the scapegoat carried away the sins of the Israelites. His death – the death of a perfectly sinless and guiltless sacrifice – completely paid the price that we owe God for our own and Adam's sins. Jesus died in our place so that we might live. (Hence the "Substitution" title.)*
>
> *We are saved when we receive Jesus as our Lord and believe in his name. Salvation is a free gift of God; no one can earn it. That means there is nothing we can do in our own power to make ourselves guiltless in God's*

A Match Made In Heaven

> sight. Even our faith is a gift – one receives no credit or reward for believing.
>
> When we believe, God counts our faith to us as righteousness, that is, he imputes some of Christ's infinite store of righteousness to the believer. Our sinfulness is not removed, just the guilt and penalty for the sin. We sinners are covered with the cloak of Christ's righteousness. When God looks upon us He doesn't see the sin still under there, only Christ's righteousness. Because God has declared us righteous, has saved us, justified us and made us His children, we can be sure we will never lose our salvation no matter what we may do.

I will show this theory is fiction. True, the rationale for the theory comes from scripture, but is founded not on scripture but upon false assumptions and an imaginative rendering of what scripture says.

I have not found a simple, clear exposition of the reasoning behind the Penal Substitution version of the message. Without that, we can't test internal consistency. But it isn't necessary that we show both internal and external consistency; the lack of either shoots down the theory. So I will ignore the question of internal consistency and show the theory is not consistent with scriptural evidence. As we agreed previously, the dataset for this task, as for the previous one, consists of the Old and New Testaments, as we have them today, in the Greek language.

The word atonement itself has an interesting history. Note first that the words in scripture now translated *atonement* were originally translated as *reconciliation*. The word atonement was invented by Tyndale and entered the English language in 1513.

Atone, the verb form, originally meant reconcile. Atone entered the language in 1593. The modern meaning of atone is *to make amends*, and of atonement is *reparation for an offense or injury*. The original meanings of the words are not the modern ones, but they are instinctively interpreted with the modern meaning by modern readers.

The following excerpt from a World Lingo article sheds useful light on the words' meanings.

> [**Begin quote**] *The word atonement gained widespread use in the sixteenth century after William Tyndale recognized that there was no direct translation of the concept into English. In order to explain the doctrine of Christ's sacrifice, which accomplished both the remission of sin and reconciliation of man to God, Tyndale invented a word that would encompass both actions. He wanted to overcome the inherent limitations of the word **reconciliation** while incorporating the aspects of **propitiation [the act of gaining or regaining the favor or goodwill of someone]** and forgiveness.*
>
> *It is interesting to note that while Tyndale labored to translate the 1526 English Bible, his proposed word comprises two parts, **at** and **onement**, which also means reconciliation, but combines it with something more.*
>
> *Although one thinks of the Jewish Fast of Yom Kippur (Day of Atonement), the Hebrew word is kaper meaning **a covering**, so one can see that **reconciliation** doesn't precisely contain all the necessary components of the word **atonement**. **Expiation** means **to atone for**. Reconciliation comes from Latin roots **re**, meaning again; **con**, meaning **with**; and ultimately, **sol**, a root meaning **seat**. Reconciliation, therefore, literally means **to sit again with**.*
>
> *While this meaning may appear sufficient, Tyndale thought that if translated as **reconciliation**, there would be a pervasive misunderstanding of the word's deeper significance to not just reconcile, but **to cover**, so the word was invented.* [**End of quote**]

A Match Made In Heaven

This discussion of the origin of 'atonement' provides an excellent example of mistaken doctrine leading to mistaken translation. Because Tyndale was looking for *guilt* in the passages he was translating, he found it where it did not exist. Jesus himself three times said words to the effect that acts committed in ignorance are not sin so do not make one guilty. Here are those verses, plus Apostle Paul's similar statement:

> *Those of the Pharisees who were with Him heard these things and said to Him, "We are not blind too, are we?" Jesus said to them, "If you were blind, you would have no sin; but since you say,* **We see***, your sin remains."* (John 9:40, 41 NASB)

> *If I had not come and spoken to them, they would not have sin, but now they have no excuse for their sin.* John 15:22 NASB

> *If I had not done among them the works which no one else did, they would not have sin; but now they have both seen and hated Me and My Father as well.* John 15:24 NASB

> *...even though I was formerly a blasphemer and a persecutor and a violent aggressor. Yet I was shown mercy because I acted ignorantly in unbelief* 1 Tim 1:13

These verses taken together clearly teach that acts committed unknowingly or unintentionally are not sin so do not make one guilty. However, any transgression of the Social Law subjects one to a curse, making it impossible for a transgressor to receive the blessing that follows obedience. Romans 2:3-16 make clear the cursing and blessing apply to all mankind, not just to those who have the Law and are under the Law.

The passages Tyndale used in developing the idea of atonement were discussing *sin offerings* by or for one who had unintentionally or unknowingly transgressed the Law. The

Hebrew word translated sin offering is *chatta'ah* (*khat-taw-aw*) which can mean, *an offence* (sometimes habitual sinfulness), *and its penalty, occasion, sacrifice, or expiation*; also (concretely) *an offender*. In the Septuagint, the word is *hamartia*, which we take to carry the same meanings. The Ceremonial Law was established to provide any of God's people who had unknowingly transgressed the Law a way to be freed from the curse. Notice that the word translated *sin offering* can refer to the penalty for transgressing the Law – cursing.

The Hebrew word translated *covering*, the second half of Tyndale's word, is **kaphar (kaw-far')**, *to cover* (specifically with bitumen); figuratively, *to expiate or condone, to placate or cancel*.

Since the word translated *cover* has alternate meaning *cancel* among others, a translation in better accord with the text would be *sin offering: an offering to cancel the penalty for unintentional sin*.

Consider too, **Lev 4:13,** *And if the whole congregation of Israel sin through ignorance, and the thing be hid from the eyes of the assembly, and they have done somewhat against any of the commandments of the LORD concerning things which should not be done, and are guilty;*

The Septuagint uses for the Hebrew word translated *sin* the Greek word *pouesosin*, which means *transgress the Law*– and uses the same word for the Hebrew word translated *guilty*. Thus the translation of the Greek text reads,

> *And if the whole congregation of Israel* **transgress the Law** *through ignorance and the thing had been hidden from the eyes of the assembly, ... which should not be done and* **have transgressed the Law**;*.*

No mention of guilt here, properly, since no guilt is involved.

A Match Made In Heaven
Tyndale, being focused on *guilt* and not having the advantages of *www.e-sword.com* and *www.biblelexicon.org*, was mistaken in looking for an element of *covering* in *reconciliation*. Yom Kippur is better understood as the feast celebrating the forgiveness of, or the cancellation of, the penalty for unintentional transgressions of the Law.

Tyndale was well wide of the mark in inventing a word that leads one astray instead of into truth. Christians would do well to expunge the word from their vocabulary and cross out every occurrence of *atonement* in their Bibles, writing in the margin, *reconciliation*.

On with the task at hand; I said I would show you the Substitution Theory is fiction, the product of man's imagination rather than analysis of scripture. The places where imagination displaced reason are these:

1. The theory is mistaken about the reason man is separated from God.

2. The theory is mistaken in teaching that Jesus died in our place – that he died the death each of us deserves to die because of our sinfulness.

3. The theory is mistaken in teaching that one person's sin or righteousness is imputed to another.

4. The theory mistakes the reason God instituted the Levitical sacrifices.

5. Some improperly see in the scapegoat a *figure* of Jesus Christ in that both *carried away* the sins of the people.

6. A mistaken interpretation of clear scriptural evidence leads to a teaching that our faith itself is a gift from God.

7. Substitution provides a distorted understanding of what it means to be saved.

Truth & Freedom

If enough of these areas are shown not to be in accord with scripture so that there is not substantial supporting evidence, that fact is evidence the theory is not credible and must be altered or abandoned. I'll address each of the elements of the theory in order, and show how their assumptions led the Reformers to faulty conclusions. You shouldn't take my word for it, but must decide for yourself whether the scriptures support their interpretations.

1. The theory mistakes the reason man is separated from God.

When the Reformers abandoned the Ransom Theory for one more to their liking, they were blinded to the fact that Jesus was not simply our savior, but first of all, our redeemer. Understanding that men are free moral agents and therefore free to choose what they will do, they understood we are responsible for the consequences of our choices, and that bad choices amount to transgressing God's law, which they understood to make one guilty. This was the foundation for teaching guilt for sin is what separates man from God.

Having ignored the clear teaching of the Bible, they invented a reason for Christ's sacrifice. We who have searched the scriptures together know the problem was **not** man's **guilt**, but **hereditary slavery imposed on mankind by Adam's foolish choice.** Given the laws He had established, God could not justly and morally take his slaves from Satan, who were by law his property.

God could not justly take another being's property, for that is forbidden by the 8th Commandment. Even He couldn't justly take from Satan and set free slaves he had legally obtained from their master. God acquired the right to free them, in a way not revealed to us, by Jesus' death on the Cross.

A Match Made In Heaven

2. **The theory is mistaken in teaching that Jesus died in our place – that he died the death that each of us deserves to die because of our sinfulness.**

The only scripture that can be said to teach directly that Jesus died **in our place** is one statement by Jesus recorded in Mark 10:45 and repeated verbatim in the Greek of Matthew 20:28. *For even the Son of Man did not come to be served, but to serve, and to give his life as a ransom (**lutron**) for (**anti**) many.*

The preposition, *anti* normally means *in place of*, as in *"an eye for (**anti**) an eye."* The translation of the preposition *anti* in that one statement is the first foundation stone of the doctrine of Substitution. But notice that Thayer's Greek-English Lexicon defines *lutron* as : *the price for redemption, ransom (paid) for slaves.* The verse clearly is speaking of purchasing/ransoming, slaves.

Thayer has for *anti*: *2. Indicating exchange, succession, for, instead of, in place of something,... **b.** of that for which any thing is given, received, endured; ... of the price of sale (or purchase): Heb xii.16:...* **"like Esau who sold his birthright for (anti) a single meal.***"*

While it is **possible** to translate *anti* as *in place of*, its meaning in Mark 10:45 surely is much closer to Thayer's **2b** indicating that the *lutron* was the **price to be paid for**, **not in place of**, many. Even if *anti* is translated *in place of*, it makes more sense to interpret it as meaning, *in place of many who could not pay the ransom themselves.*

Clearly Jesus was telling the disciples he would be their **ransom payer**, not **die the death men deserve to die.** The fact that *anti* can reasonably be translated with a meaning following naturally from the idea of ransom speaks loudly against using it in the way the theory does.

Truth & Freedom

Having decided the verse teaches substitution, those who promote the theory look around for supporting evidence. They claim to find that evidence in a few verses that use another Greek word translated *for, huper*.

Thayer has for *huper*, **:I. 2.** *for, i.e. for one's safety, for one's advantage, or benefit. ... Since what is done for one's advantage frequently cannot be done without acting in his stead ... we easily understand how* **huper***, like the Latin pro and our for comes to signify* **3.** *In the place of, instead of, (which is more precisely expressed by* **anti***) ... Since anything whether of an active or passive character which is undertaken on behalf of a person or thing is taken 'on account of' that person or thing,* **huper** *is used* **4.** *Of the impelling or moving cause; on account of, for the sake of any person or thing.* **6.** *In the NT mss., as in the prof(ane) auth(ors) also, the prepositions* **huper** *and* **peri** *are confounded. ... This occurs in the following pass(ages)...* Gal. 1:4.

K. S. Wuest translates *huper* as *on behalf of* or *in behalf of* in passages describing what Jesus did for us. One excellent example is found in Romans 5:6-8:

> *You see, at just the right time, when we were still powerless, Christ died for (***huper***) the ungodly. Very rarely will anyone die for (***huper***) a righteous man, though for (***huper***) a good man someone might possibly dare to die. But God demonstrates his own love for us in this: While we were still sinners, Christ died for (***huper***) us.* (NIV)

Here's Wuest's expanded translation:

> *For when we were yet without strength, in a strategic season, Christ* **instead of and in behalf of** *those who do not have reverence for God and are devoid of piety, died; for very rarely in behalf of a righteous man will anyone die, yet perhaps in behalf of a good man, a*

A Match Made In Heaven

> *person would even dare to die. But God is constantly proving His own love to us because while we were yet sinners, Christ in behalf of us died.*

Wuest avoided the translation problem by not deciding between the meanings, considering both to be valid. These verses are not unquestionable evidence for substitution instead of ransom.

The NIV translates Galatians 3:13 as

> *Christ redeemed us from the curse of the law by becoming a curse for (huper) us, for it is written, 'Cursed is everyone who is hung on a tree.'*

This verse has given me no end of trouble because I could not understand how Christ could have become a curse. The Old Testament verse quoted does not say everyone hung on a tree **becomes** a curse, but **is** cursed. That's what the verse should say about Christ. I learned a lot about Greek participles in trying to sort this out, which I guess is a good thing. But there is no getting around it – the Greek does say Christ became (or was made) a curse for us.

Thankfully, Thayer's Greek-English Lexicon of the New Testament has a note on the verse; *abstract for the concrete, one in whom the curse is exhibited, i.e. undergoing the appointed penalty of cursing.*

A possible translation of this troubling verse might be, *Christ redeemed us from the curse of the law and while doing so became accursed for us (on our behalf), for it is written...* Huper cannot reasonably mean *in our place* here because sinful man was already under the curse imposed by the law, and that curse is still in effect for those who transgress the Social Law.

Other verses said definitely to teach substitution are John 10:50 – *...nor do you take into account that it is expedient for you that one man die for* **(huper)** *the people, and that the whole nation* *not perish*, Gal 1:4 – *Who gave himself for (huper/peri) our sins so that He might rescue us out from this present pernicious age, according to the will of our God and Father.* (Wuest) – and 2 Cor. 5:14, 15 – *For (gar) Christ's love compels us, because we are convinced that one died for (**huper**) all, and therefore all died. And he died for (**huper**) all, that those who live should no longer live for themselves, but for him who died for (**huper**) them and was raised again.* (NIV).

Huper in John 10:50 can reasonably be translated as in place of (the people dying). But here we see innocent people dying if another innocent person does not die. This cannot be taken as showing Jesus died in place of people who deserve to die. Galatians 1:4 is not convincingly translated *in place of* for the usual reasons, and loses further credibility in that the majority of the source manuscripts use *peri* instead of *huper*.

None of these verses clearly and unambiguously teach substitution. There is no substantial evidence supporting the idea that Christ died the death all mankind deserves to die. The evidence strongly supports the conclusion that Christ died **in/on our behalf**, not in our place.

3.   The theory is mistaken in teaching that one person's sin or righteousness is imputed to another.

This second foundation stone of Substitution theory is not supported by scripture. Apparently those who created the theory looked at 2 Cor 5:21 – *God made him who had no sin to be sin for us, so that in him we might become the righteousness of God* (NIV) – and asked themselves, "How can God have made Christ sin for us?"

They found their answer in Romans 4, where Paul discusses God's counting Abram's faith to him as righteousness. The same word translated counting, counted is also translated imputing, imputed in that chapter.

A Match Made In Heaven
The reasoning is something like this:

> *God **imputed** Abraham's faith to him as righteousness. By analogy, God made Him who knew no sin to be sin by **imputing** the sins of the world to Him. It makes sense, then, that Christ could die in our place, die the death we deserve to die because of our sin, becoming an acceptable sacrifice for sins for which we could make no acceptable sacrifice ourselves. Thus, Jesus carried away on the cross all the sins of all humans in all ages.*
>
> *Not only that, we see how it is that we become guilty of Adam's sin – God **imputes** Adam's sin to each of us, adding the guilt for original sin to whatever guilt we have accumulated for ourselves. So even if there were such a thing as a totally right-living descendant of Adam, he or she would still be guilty of sin because God **imputes** Adam's sin to all his descendants.*
>
> *(Those who see the gross injustice of God doing that rely on the **bad seed** idea – all creation was cursed by Adam's sin, including Adam's seed. We were **in Adam's loins** when he was cursed for sinning the great sin and therefore we carry his sin in our genes.)*

[You will recall that God did not act in anger toward Adam and Eve after their sin, but in love provided them with clothing and locked them away from the Tree of Life to prevent them from becoming eternally enslaved to Satan. God did not curse them; He was protecting them from the fruit of their own folly.]

> *Furthermore, we can understand how we become **the righteousness of God in him**. When we believe in Christ – that he is God's son, and that he took our place on the cross – God **imputes** some of Christ's infinite store of righteousness to each of us.*

Thus was created a neat little fiction, a foundation upon which was built a theology that explains (in their sight) all of the New Testament. There are at least three difficulties with this theory:

>**a.** Neither the Old nor the New Testament teaches that any person's sin or righteousness is imputed to another person. In every case where the word is used, what is imputed to a person already belongs to that person.
>
>**b.** The process described in Romans 4, by which God imputed Abraham's faith to him as righteousness, is parallel to the Roman Catholic process of beatification – the *making* of a Saint. The church does not **make** one a Saint, it **officially recognizes the fact** that the way he lived his life **shows he was** a saint.
>
>We should understand Romans chapter 4 that way. In counting Abraham righteous because of his faith, God was not **making** him righteous, but was officially recognizing that he **was in fact** righteous, that fact having been demonstrated by his faith.
>
>**c.** The presentation ignores the fact that the Hebrew word for sin, translated into Greek by *hamartia* and used in 2 Cor. 5:21, can mean *the offense, its occasion, or its penalty, sacrifice or expiation*, a fact that surely was known by the well educated Paul.

The verse cannot mean that God made Jesus our offenses themselves, or the occasion of our sins, or the penalty for our sins, since none of those translations makes sense. We are left with the verse teaching that God made Jesus the sacrifice that **removes the consequences** of sin.

Clearly, that is what the verse means. It simply says, *God made him who was without offense to be the sacrifice that removes the consequence of sin* (i.e. slavery and/or cursing), *in our behalf, so that in him we might become the righteousness of*

A Match Made In Heaven

God. This is not just an idea I stumbled across; the NIV text note suggests something like this as an alternate translation.

In summary: Scripture nowhere teaches that God transfers sin or righteousness from one person to another. Instead, the verses alleged to teach such transfers actually teach God formally recognizes what already exists. Even the perceived need for teaching such a transfer vanishes when a single verse – 2 Cor.5:21 – is properly translated. There is no scriptural basis for the doctrinal position that God transfers – imputes – any person's sin or righteousness to another.

4.   The theory mistakes the reason the Levitical sacrifices were instituted. Careful reading of any decent translation shows that the sacrifices were instituted to provide a way for God's people who **inadvertently** transgressed God's Laws, to remove from themselves the curse the Law imposes for any breach. The Law in the cases addressed by the sacrifices had nothing to do with guilt, because there was no guilt, as Jesus' own words clearly show.

5.   Some improperly see in the scapegoat a figure of Jesus Christ in that both carried away the sins of the people. That symbolism does not accurately parallel Jesus' redeeming act, since the scapegoat was not sacrificially killed, but was driven away from the camp into the wilderness.

6.   A mistaken interpretation of clear scriptural evidence leads to a teaching that our faith itself is a gift from God. Ephesians 2:8: *For by grace are ye saved through faith; and that not of yourselves: it is the gift of God* is mistakenly interpreted by some who teach God's gift in this verse is faith. The rules of Greek grammar – a pronoun must agree with its antecedent in case, number and gender – make it impossible to interpret the verse that way.

Faith is genitive case, singular number and feminine gender. The demonstrative pronoun translated *that* is nominative case, singular number and neuter gender. *That* cannot refer to *faith*; so it must refer to another noun. The noun to which *that* refers must be *the gift*, the only nominative, singular, neuter noun in the verse. Wuest (Ephesians in the Greek New Testament for the English Reader p. 69) supplies *salvation* as the antecedent of *that* – salvation is the gift of God.

[Understand, please, I'm not saying faith is not a gift from God, just that this verse doesn't teach it is. I haven't examined that question, so have no opinion on the matter.]

7. Substitution provides a distorted understanding of what it means to be saved. When the Reformers decided redemption rescued mankind from the consequences of sin, they lost the essential meaning of *redemption*. As a result, the word is often used today as having essentially the same meaning as *salvation*; the two sometimes being used interchangeably. I'll not here go further into what it means to be saved, but will take that up in the next chapter.

Redemption translating *lutrosis* should be applied only to Christ's self sacrificial act that transferred ownership of Satan's slaves to God. *Apolutrosis*, also translated by *redemption*, is another matter. Thayer has for the word, *I. of any kind of separation of one thing from another by which the union or fellowship of the two is destroyed. V. in composition, apo indicates separation, liberation, cessation, departure ...finishing and completion.* Its basic meaning, and Paul's use of the word seem to indicate a much fuller, finished and completed deliverance than ransom indicated by *lutorsis*. The verses where the word is used, which you may want to review, are listed in Chapter IV.

To summarize, the widely accepted Penal Substitution Theory of Atonement is but weakly supported by scriptural evidence. The support for the theory consists of a few scriptures that can and almost certainly should be interpreted differently. Further, the fact that scripture clearly shows Christ died to transfer

A Match Made In Heaven

Satan's slaves from his ownership to God's, is the incompatible evidence that proves the theory should not be taken seriously.

Substitution is not a proper theory, but a work of fiction. Being built on fictional ideas; it is unworthy of belief by reasonable people and must be rejected.

The Satisfaction Theory of Atonement created by Anselm and adopted first by Luther and later by the Roman Catholic Church has even less support in scripture. Advocates for the theory start with assumptions similar to those the other Reformers did, and that in itself is enough to assure its incredibility.

Suffice it to say that I have found not a single scripture that teaches God required the death of any man, let alone a perfectly sinless and infinitely worthy one, to satisfy a sin debt. Substitution hangs by a single thin thread; the Satisfaction Theory, lacking even the flimsiest of gossamers, floats itself entirely on man's far too fallible imagination.

I realize that I have here pulled the scaffolding from under many good and honest believers in Christ, who have labored in what they thought was absolute security in the upper reaches of the lofty structures created by the Reformers and their contemporaries. I tried in the beginning to provide parachutes to slow their descent and ease their landing on the hard ground of reality. I will present a little later an outline of what that reality is like, and what it means for those who are trusting in their Creator God, His Redeeming Son, and His Instructing, Convicting, and Sustaining Spirit. There you will find that man is much less sinful and God much less condemning than the Reformers imagined either to be.

A Match Made In Heaven
CHAPTER VI.

Implications

Chapters I. through V. presented the essence of what I have to share on the subject of learning truth and protecting oneself from propaganda. While my approach can surely be improved upon, learning and practicing what is presented there will give you a good start on the path to becoming the free man or woman you want to be. Now I will leave that central message and devote a couple of chapters to discussing some of the implications of what we have learned about the Bible message.

I will be pleased if all you who have read thus far will continue with me to the end, but it you are not inclined to do that, I encourage you to not leave without first reading Appendix I and Appendix II. You will find both of them interesting and instructive. For those still with me, follow along while we look a bit at a question that has puzzled believers for centuries.

Why Did Jesus Die?

We've seen the shortcomings of accepted atonement theories and we know Christ's death rescued us from slavery to Satan, now we are left with the question, "What is different now that we are no longer Satan's slaves, but belong to God?"

We've seen that we are God's slaves, his property. But **2000** years of history since Jesus died convinces us God does not treat us as slaves. In fact, it appears that He permits us the utmost freedom to choose what we believe and how we live. This is not how the World treats slaves, but it is the way God treated Adam in the beginning. It seems then that Jesus' death must have restored to man the freedom that Adam lost for all mankind.

In chapter IV we concluded that God intended Adam to live forever. Was this privilege restored in the New Testament? It seems obvious that it was at least made possible for those who so choose to enjoy that blessing. The Greek word for life appears 134 times in 126 verses of the New Testament, 47 of which are in the phrase "eternal life". Many of the remaining verses also speak of eternal life without using that expression. There is no question that the New Testament teaches "*all who receive Him, who believe on His name*" will receive everlasting life as a consequence of becoming "*children of God*" [John 1:12]

The New Testament also teaches that Christ came to save us. What does that mean? The Greek word is *sozo*, meaning to *save, rescue or preserve* someone from danger or destruction. The word is translated in various ways depending on the context, e.g., cured an illness, but the basic meaning remains the same.

If this is a valid understanding of what the word means, then the essential idea is that those who receive and believe Jesus is the Christ, their Savior, will be saved from ultimate destruction, which is death. So here again we are taught that God intends His children to live forever. And if it is true that all must pass through physical death to enter eternal life, then that suggests to me that salvation is not a one time salvation event but a process that will be complete only when we see Jesus face to face.

And we see, too, that just as Adam walked and talked with God, we may also. For He has sent the Holy Spirit to commune with our spirits, so that *We have the mind of Christ.* (1 Cor 2:16) We may, and many do, converse with Him daily, often many times throughout the day, receiving instruction, admonition, encouragement, comfort; all the good fruits the Spirit blesses us with. Blessing piled upon blessing is the lot of those who emulate our Savior, Jesus Christ.

Another thing before leaving this too short and sketchy chapter: how shall we understand the *wrath of God*? The Greek word is

A Match Made In Heaven

orge, and is very often translated *anger, wrath*. The basic meaning of the word is strong emotion, whether anger, desire, love, etc. Thayer suggests a possible meaning of wrath in John 3:35 ... *and he that believeth not the Son shall not see life, but the **wrath** of God abideth upon him* as being *justifiable abhorrence*. That is, God will **justifiably abhor** those who decline His gracious offer of eternal life by failing to honor the heroic self sacrifice of His Son. Abhorrence is a really strong emotion, don't you agree?

Then I ask, *How can a just and loving God sentence anyone to eternal punishment in Hell?* There are two parts to the answer: God cannot justly let those who dishonor His Son share the reward of those who do honor Him. And it is not clear to me as I write this that unbelievers **will** suffer **eternal** torment.

The word translated *Hell* in the New Testament is everywhere *gehenna*, the Greek word for the valley of *Hinnom*, the place where Jerusalem's refuse was taken to be disposed of, a place where the fire never went out and the worms never died. The plain meaning is that those who dishonor Christ will be thrown out with the garbage, not necessarily that they will suffer eternal torment. But other verses refer to eternal, unquenchable fire, and to wailing and gnashing of teeth, which may point to eternal punishment in spite of what I'd like to believe.

For now, I take the final destination of unbelievers to be the place of burning, the place where natural action turns their remains to the dust from which they came. But until all those other verses are studied and thoroughly understood, it would be foolish to take this as the whole teaching on the crucial question of the final destiny of God's enemies.

I can't resist the temptation to share with you one final thought. The debate with atheists about the existence or non existence of God has degenerated into a shouting match, with each side loudly proclaiming the other cannot prove its position. That certainly is true of the atheist position, for they are on solid ground.

Atheists base their lives on the belief that no god exists, and most apply this specifically to the Judeo-Christian God. Logic requires anyone challenging that position to provide evidence for the existence of such a God; atheists have stated their position and it is up to challengers to prove they are wrong. Believers, on the other hand say God exists, to which atheists properly respond, "Prove it!"

Let me use this crude example to explain the situation: Two people, Atheist and Believer are disputing. Atheist points to a corked glass bottle sitting on the counter and says, "That bottle is empty." Believer says, "No, that bottle is full of an invisible substance, called air." Atheist responds, "I don't see any air. Prove the bottle is full of air." Believer takes a hair dryer, heats the bottle, the air expands and blows the cork out of the bottle, proving the bottle was not empty.

Atheist, not wanting to concede, says, "That doesn't prove anything, it was the heat that blew the cork out of the bottle." So believer hooks a vacuum pump to the bottle, pulls the air out of the bottle using it to inflate a balloon to show something really did come out of the bottle then applies heat. The cork doesn't pop out of the bottle no matter how much heat is applied. The two experiments prove beyond dispute that the bottle did contain an invisible substance called air.

We are in the same situation. We are challenged to prove the existence of an invisible God, and our response must be to show by the results of our actions that God exists. The ball is in our court. If we are to convince unbelievers that God exists, we must conduct an experiment that shows certain actions result in effects that are absent when the actions are absent.

Members of the Body of Christ – a subset of those who profess belief in God and His Son – routinely experience just such

A Match Made In Heaven

effects while others do not. The challenge is to demonstrate in a controlled experiment that those who do not now experience those effects will begin to experience them when they begin to live God's way. Here is how I suggest we go about this:

> Scripture presents many examples of God's ability to control physical processes. Examples from the Old Testament include parting the Red Sea and later the Jordan River so the people could cross over, stopping the sun in the sky so Joshua's forces could completely destroy the enemy before nightfall and causing the shadow to move backward down the stairway to confirm the answer to Hezekiah's prayer. Examples from the New Testament include Jesus walking on water, calming the storm, changing water to wine, feeding the five thousand, raising Lazarus and rising from death himself.
>
> These verses clearly teach God is able to make things happen that science says are impossible because that would violate the natural laws that control how things happen. As far as science is concerned, it is impossible for those scripture stores to be true. Of course, there is no direct way to test those ancient happenings, but what if, as the Bible seems to teach, God might again perform that kind of miracle when mankind earns the right to be blessed as He promised He would bless?
>
> Such a teaching can be tested by an experiment, and if what the teaching predicts occurs as predicted, that is evidence for the Bible's reliability and for God's existence. I remind those whose hackles rose at the thought of a person earning a right to be blessed that I'm not talking about salvation here, but just plain, everyday blessing.

Here is the reasoning behind the suggestion:

1. Scripture clearly teaches God can miraculously control physical events.

2. Scripture also teaches that God will bless those who obey His Social Laws, and **curse** those who do not.

3. As assumed in Chapter IV., the Social Laws govern all thinking beings just like natural laws govern all material things.

4. Romans chapters 1 and 2 make it clear that the social law applies to all men, believers and unbelievers alike, that they should know that God exists because they can clearly see proof of that, and that they are cursed with "tribulation and anguish" by their unbelief.

5. I take *Cursing* to mean not active hostility but simply the absence of *blessing*, implying that those currently cursed will begin to be blessed when they begin to obey the Social Law.

6. Romans 8: 18-23 clearly teach that all creation was cursed when Adam sinned, and presumably remains cursed because of man's sins.

7. Because God curses disobedience and blesses obedience, both the manmade troubles that plague mankind and the current epidemic of natural disasters will be removed when some majority of mankind acknowledges God's social laws and begins to obey them.

8. This is a proposition that can be falsified, and thus qualifies as a valid scientific test.

9. If falsified, the experiment tells us nothing about God's existence but does show our understanding of the meaning of the quoted scriptures is invalid.

A Match Made In Heaven

10. If the experiment yields the predicted results, that shows our understanding is valid. And since that understanding is based on statements attributed to the Judeo-Christian God that provides positive evidence of His existence, thus satisfying atheists' demands for scientific evidence that God exists.

It will be interesting to see how atheists respond to this challenge since the theory cannot be tested without their beginning to act in ways the Bible says they must act to receive the promised benefits of their actions. If they decline to accept the challenge, they can logically blame only themselves for each manmade and natural disaster that occurs.

If they are forced by public pressure to take the challenge seriously, they will surely attempt to show scriptures do not teach this. And that would mean they would have to engage in serious scripture study, which would not be a bad thing for atheists or for believers. And this applies not just to atheists but to everybody, including Christians, many of whom do not know biblical truth but only what they have been taught by others who too often have been at best misled by their teachers, or who knowingly twist the scriptures to secure for themselves benefits from those they deceive.

Pushing society to attempt the experiment, while holding unbelievers responsible for every bad thing, cannot be bad for anyone. If a significant portion of the population begins to treat others with Christian love, that will go far toward eliminating many of the planets ills. If as the experiment suggests, God will heal the planet as well, thus proving He is God, that will be the second greatest blessing this old world could ever hope to know!

This is a short chapter, asking several questions but providing no answers, only suggestions. Finding those answers is left as an exercise for you. You know how to do it; you have been given tools and examples that show you how to do it. All that is needed is for you to begin and to quit only when you are satisfied that you have the answers. I urge you to begin while what you've read is still fresh in your mind, and I caution you against undertaking this challenge by yourself. Find another of like mind, or several others, and make this a joint project.

As iron sharpens iron, so one man sharpens another; a cord of three strands is not easily broken.

A Match Made In Heaven
CHAPTER VII.

The Resuscitated Church

Assuming the conclusions reached herein – especially those of Chapters III., IV. and V. – stand up to scrutiny. let's take a look at how the Church might look when the life strangling doctrinal errors have been sucked out and life giving truth pumped in. *Resuscitated* (*revived from apparent death or unconsciousness*) fitly portrays the Church that will displace today's feeble church, with its tens of thousands of competing fragments each living in isolation from all others. Please don't take what follows as established truth, I here offer only suggestions.

I'll begin by recording some assumptions I believe to be true, only a few of which I have rigorously tested:

1.   **God created Adam a free man** who would care for His Garden and walk and talk with Him in the cool of the day, a free man, able to choose what he would do, how he would live and whom he would believe and obey.

2.   Being free is like being pregnant **– you are or you are not.**

3.   Christ redeemed the Gentiles, transferring them from Satan's ownership to God's, elevating them to the position Israel has occupied for millennia. **Today all people are God's People.** This emphatically **does not** mean the Church has replaced Israel as the apple of God's eye.

4.   **God desires all to be saved.** All will be saved if they believe in Jesus and receive Him as their Savior and Messiah. He has foreknowledge of the actions and attitudes of those who will be saved, but not their names, their deeds and their natures. The Reformers' idea that man is totally depraved and

unable to do the smallest thing to gain God's favor has no support in scripture.

5.   **God is at peace with man**; He no longer makes war against some people to protect His People; all people are His people.

6.   **The Ceremonial Law and the Aaronic priesthood are no more**; Jesus Christ, the new High Priest, is the sole Mediator between God and man and the new Mercy Seat to which man must go for cleansing from the curse that comes with transgressing the Law.

7.   **The Social Law remains in effect**; obedience is blessed, disobedience is cursed. Transgressions are pardoned and the curse removed when one goes to Christ, confesses his sins and asks forgiveness. Israel, misled by Rabbis who with the best of intentions prevented them from turning to Christ for pardon, remains to this day under the curse of the Social Law.

8.   The Law no longer requires stoning people who willfully and consistently rebel against it. That seems to have passed away along with the Ceremonial Law. I don't know whether God's People remain responsible for removing rebels from among their number.

9.   God intends for believers to be *conformed to the image of His Son* (Rom 8:29); *who will transform the body of our humble state into conformity with the body of His glory* (Phil3:21)

Let's add to these assumptions a **working hypothesis: God is assembling a multitude of free men and women who have been recreated in the image of pre-Fall Adam – God's equal in sovereignty and in nothing else – their actions and attitudes conformed to those of the second Adam, Jesus Christ.**

I won't show the thought process that led to an understanding

A Match Made In Heaven

of how this transforming and conforming are accomplished, just cite some scriptures that may help us understand how it is done.

John 1:12 *But as many as received Him, to them he gave the right to become the children of God, to those who believe in his name*, shows being saved is a process, not an instantaneous event. "Being made" might be done instantly; "becoming" is a process extending over time and involving multiple steps.

Rom 10:9 tells us the process begins when we *confess with our mouth, Jesus is Lord and believe in our hearts God raised Him from the dead.*

Galatians 3:26 and **1 John 3:1** show us the result of the *becoming* of John 1:12: *For ye are all the children of God by faith in Christ Jesus* and *How great is the love the Father has lavished on us, that we should be called children of God! And that is what we are.*

Heb 5:12, 13 indicates all begin the process as babes in the Lord, not capable of handling the deeper things of God, but only the basics – *For though by this time you ought to be teachers, you have need again for someone to teach you the elementary principles of the oracles of God, and you have come to need milk and not solid food. For everyone who partakes only of milk is not accustomed to the word of righteousness, for he is an infant.*

Gal 4:1, 2 points out infants, and all the immature, are not capable of learning for themselves; they need tutors and guardians until their father knows they are sufficiently mature to make their own decisions. *Now I say, as long as the heir is a child, he does not differ at all from a slave although he is owner of everything, but he is under guardians and managers until the date set by the father.*

Gal 4:5-7 add important information: *so that He might redeem those who were under the Law, that we might receive the adoption as sons. Because you are sons, God has sent forth the Spirit of His Son into our hearts, crying, 'Abba! Father!' Therefore you are no longer a slave, but a son; and if a son, then an heir through God.*

K. S. Wuest interprets Galatians 4:5 as teaching adoption is the means God uses to establish the believer as a free, mature member of His family:

*(Christ) died under law, and in His resurrection, was raised into a realm where law as a legalistic system does not exist. This He did, in order that He might not only deliver us from the law but also raise believers with Himself into a realm where law does not operate. Instead therefore of being children (immature ones, **nepios**) under law, we became adult sons (**huios**) under grace. We received the adoption of sons.*

*This expression in the Greek is literally, in order that we might receive the **adult son-placing**. We could paraphrase it in order that we might be placed as adult sons. Thus we have presented to us the status of a person under grace as compared to that of a person under law. The latter is in his minority, the former in his majority, the latter treated like a minor, the former like an adult.* (Galatians in the Greek New Testament, p. **116**)

This formulation recognizes the new Christian, though an heir is a babe in Christ, and is still subject to the Social Law and the cursing and blessing of Deuteronomy chapters **27** and **28**. He will remain so until the Father recognizes he has matured to the point that he automatically chooses blessing.

At that point, he is manumitted – a fancy term that means *is set free* – from dependence on blessing and cursing to teach him right from wrong. He **knows** right from wrong, and consistently chooses the right.

A Match Made In Heaven

1 John 2:12-14 indicate three levels of maturity, *little children*, *young men* and *fathers*. Galatians chapter 4 shows the progression from the heir still under the law and tutors and managers, to the adoption of a son, *huios*. At this point in his development, he is John's *young man*. None of this means he cannot sin. *Scripture* clearly teaches *all have sinned and fall short of the glory of God*, and *If we say we have no sin, we deceive ourselves, and the truth is not in us.* **Willfully ignoring the law is a sign one is still a babe in Christ, still under the schoolmaster, still subject to blessing and cursing, not to be entrusted with the spiritual lives of others.**

Following the figure to its logical conclusion, the young man continues walking through life, communing with God through the Holy Spirit, growing with each new experience. He is involved in ministry, recognizing that God wants His people to be busy edifying – building up – His church, the Body of Christ. As he grows and matures, he takes on more responsible ministries, still growing and learning as his transformation continues.

At some point, this *young man* finds he has been transformed into what John calls a *father*. He knows intimately and is a constant companion of *Him who is from the beginning* – Christ Jesus. He has been, in the language of Romans **8:29**, (substantially) *conformed to the image of His Son* that being the ultimate goal of any person's walk with God.

This does not mean anyone achieves perfection in this life. Saint Paul was about as saintly as any human can be. If he can say, *Not ... that I am already perfected* (Phil **3:12**) near the end of his life, how likely is it that any now living can truthfully make that claim? The *father*, like our example Paul, *forgetting what lies behind and reaching forward to what lies ahead, (presses) on toward the goal.* Phil **3:13,14** NASB. The goal of the *father* is, as it was Paul's, to finish well.

Truth & Freedom

We don't see many Christians of that kind today, nor do we see many pressing ahead to reach that goal. Why is that? Isn't it because the Christian Church, distracted by faulty doctrines and too filled with love for the world, has left the mission God assigned to it, chasing after other things? Are there any living today who might fit that description of a *father*. If there are any, they almost certainly will, except for rare exceptions, be found in the Orthodox churches, where, if they live up to their statements, men's lives are still guided by Holy Scripture and Holy Tradition.

So here, I suggest, is a short version of the scripture message about the salvation God intends for all who believe on His Son.

1. We are born belonging to God, He owns us, He is our Master, our Sovereign.

2. Though He is our Sovereign, He allows us the freedom to choose what we will believe and what we will do.

3. Up until the time we believe, His Social Law guides and teaches us through its cursing and blessing.

4. When we hear the truth about Jesus and believe, we begin, as babes in Christ, the process of becoming conformed to the likeness of His Son, Jesus.

5. So long as we are babes and spiritually immature, we remain under the tutelage of the Law with its blessing and cursing. We rely on the promise of 1 John 1:9, *If we confess our sins, He is faithful and just to forgive our sins and cleanse us from all unrighteousness*, to remove the curse and restore the blessing.

6. At some point, if we diligently pursue the path set before us, we are set free from the Law, having reached spiritual maturity.

A Match Made In Heaven

7. The spiritually mature persists in following the path God sets before him, growing in faith and wisdom until he is substantially conformed to the image of Jesus.

8. Those substantially conformed to Jesus' image are the Fathers of the church, her teachers and leaders.

9. When their time on earth is ended, the Fathers, like all believers, are taken to heaven, where the conforming process is completed.

Let's now look briefly at how it might look if these ideas are read, confirmed and implemented in the Christian Churches. First, it is certain that churches who see their calling as producing men and women conformed to the image of Christ Jesus will organize their doctrines and practices much closer to those of the Orthodox churches. Orthodoxy has for two millennia accepted that their goal is **theosis**, translated as *god making*, and understood by Orthodoxy to mean *conforming people to the image of Christ*.

Orthodoxy does not search the scriptures to create doctrines, but contents itself with the doctrine formalized as the Nicene Creed in the 325 A. D. Ecumenical Council of Nicea, and expanded in the 381 A. D. Council. Here is the translation of the Creed used by the Orthodox Church in America:

> *I believe in one God the Father almighty, Maker of heaven and earth, and of all things visible and invisible.*
>
> *And in one Lord Jesus Christ, the Son of God, the only-begotten, begotten of the Father before all ages; Light of Light, true God of true God, begotten, not made, of one essence with the Father, by whom all things were made.*
>
> *Who for us men and for our salvation came down from heaven, and was incarnate of the Holy Spirit and the Virgin Mary, and became man; and was crucified also*

for us under Pontius Pilate, and suffered and was buried; and the third day He rose again according to the Scriptures; and ascended into heaven and sits at the right hand of the Father.

And He shall come again with glory to judge the living and the dead; of His kingdom there shall be no end.

And in the Holy Spirit, the Lord, the Giver of life, Who proceedeth from the Father, Who with the Father and the Son together is worshipped and glorified, Who spoke by the prophets.

In one Holy Catholic and Apostolic Church;

I confess one baptism for the forgiveness of sins;

I look for the resurrection of the dead and the life of the age to come. Amen.

Orthodoxy is not guided solely by doctrine, however, Holy Tradition – said to enshrine the beliefs and practices handed down by the Apostles and Church Fathers – exerts a strong influence as well. Some of Orthodoxy's traditions and practices seem strange, even repugnant, to people coming out of Protestantism. Among them are the use of icons, the veneration of and praying to the saints and the Virgin Mary, the belief in the eternal virginity of Mary, and the actual presence of the body and blood of Jesus in the communion wafer and wine.

Those procedural issues are based on tradition, not on scripture. Perhaps an emerging Resuscitated Church may be received into fellowship with Orthodoxy when all agree to accept others whose doctrines and practices are reliably extracted from scripture.

Perhaps all can agree that the Holy Spirit assured the **essentials** of Tradition were included in the canonical scriptures and what

A Match Made In Heaven

is now called Holy Tradition deals with important but not essential practices.

Perhaps someday the millennium-long fracture in Christian unity will be healed when the surviving four branches of Orthodoxy recognize a new Western Orthodoxy has replaced apostate Rome as the Church of the West.

A dream, yes! Why should those who love God and His Book not dream that He will use His People to spread His Word and His Truth about His Salvation through His Son over His Creation, *as the waters cover the sea*?

The first verse of an old hymn, by one unknown to me, sums up the dream this author has for himself and his loved ones in the world and the Church to come.

> *My God and I walk in the fields together*
> *We **walk** and talk as good **friends** should and do*
> *We clasp our hands, our voices ring with laughter*
> *My God and I walk through the meadow's dew*
> *We clasp our hands, our voices ring with laughter*
> *My God and I walk through the meadow's dew*

It would be fun to sit here with you, dreaming about what lies ahead for us and for the church, but we can't forget why we are here. We are talking together about the need to know truth, how to find it and how to know we've found it. John 8: 31, 32 summarize it well, Jesus speaking; *If you hold to my teaching, you are really my disciples. Then you will know the truth, and the truth will set you free.* (NIV) There you are; Jesus' disciples will know the truth and their holding to His teaching is their evidence they do know it. And they can be supremely confident knowing truth will set them free.

We've come a long way toward knowing the truth the Bible has for us. We have seen that truth is missing from current teaching in nearly all Christendom. We've seen that mistaken doctrines place false emphasis on activities different from what Christians should be concerned about. We've found that the true message describes not a wrathful, offended God, but a loving God who wants the best for His People, but who does not impose His will upon any of them.

We've come this long way because we have learned to use tools that help us decide who to believe and what to believe, so we are much further along the path to true freedom than when we started this study. We are confident we will attain to the ultimate freedom God has for His People in this world if we faithfully apply these tools to test anything and everything others try to impose upon us.

I am convinced God wants to walk and talk with His People as friends and companions, sovereign men and women who walk with Him because they know it is in their best interest to do so. They will do that not because He tells them they must, imposing His will upon them, but because they have learned through experience that He loves them, wants only good for them, and is perfectly capable of giving them their heart's desires. Switching to the first person, we needn't worry that what we desire is outside His will for us if we are walking in the truth He has preserved for us in His Book.

Knowing scriptural truth is not all that is needed if we are to be free. We must be able to cut through the manmade propaganda aimed at controlling us, taking our money and our freedom. We have the tools for doing that. We have a standard for truth, the Holy Scriptures. It is true that finding those other truths is harder than finding what's in God's word, but it's not impossible. We are not alone; we have the Holy Spirit, who teaches us not just God's truth, but all truth.

And we have an ever increasing crowd of brothers and sisters travelling the same path toward truth, who can and will come alongside to encourage and assist. We who walk this path are not competitors, not vying for position, not seeking for

A Match Made In Heaven

ourselves a precious one of a tiny few rewards. We walk as companions, assisting each other as we struggle together to reach a goal that holds infinitely many rewards; no one needs to struggle to get ahead, forcing his way through the crowd; all will receive the reward God has for each of us, no matter when or by what path we reach the goal God sets before us.

Now, before I leave you, may I ask you one more really, really hard question: Would you be willing, as Saint Paul said he was, to give up the promise of eternal life for yourself if by doing so you could ensure that God's still lost people, the apple of His eye, the Jews, would acquire eternal life if you did so? To me, this is an almost unanswerable question.

How can I give up this *Pearl of Great Price* that I have striven so many years to understand and to receive? Give up the greatest blessing ever bestowed upon men? If God assured me that millions of His people, even a hundred, even ten would know eternal life if I gave up mine so they could have theirs, could I do it? Surely I and you too, would say *yes* to God, perhaps fearing that by disappointing Him in that you'd lose your salvation anyway.

I don't expect God to ask us to make that sacrifice, but I wish to have the strength to say *yes* if He does ask it of me. In the meantime, will you please join me in praying that God will see his *peculiar people*, the *apple of His eye*, cast off their blinders, receive the Truth, and come to Jesus for salvation and life eternal? I feel certain that would please God perhaps even more than offering to give up our lives in exchange for theirs.

In this chapter, unlike chapters IV. and V., I've made no attempt to establish the credibility of the statements made. Instead I have made some suggestions about what may be true, and how the church may be reconfigured to permit the centuries-long divisions to be healed. Those suggestions should not be given even token credence until they have been subjected to the rigorous scrutiny described in Chapter III. In fact, nothing in this book should be blindly accepted, no matter how detailed my analysis may have been. Remember the atheist's 11th Commandment – **Question Everything!**

May Our Wonderful, Loving God Richly Bless all who read these words and take their message to heart!

A Match Made In Heaven
APPENDIX I.

Introduction to "The Ten Commandments of Propaganda"

[**Editor's note**: *I have indulged one of my personal preferences by dividing this* **Introduction** *into paragraphs of three to five sentences for easier reading, but have otherwise tried to present the material exactly as it appears in the document I have on my Kindle in April, 2013.*]

You have already been worked in a subtle way. How? Although the title of this book is The Ten Commandments of Propaganda, you will actually find eleven commandments here, and much other information beside. The reference to the Ten Commandments accesses something already stored in your brain, waiting. The title calls and activates it with virtually no effort on your part.

In an instant you already understand pretty much the whole drift of a fairly complicated concept that I am proposing. You know that you have encountered a set of precepts, shalts and shalt-nots, designed to guide thought and behavior. And by merely understanding all this, you are now well on the way to being persuaded of what I will have to say, for to understand is perhaps half way to being persuaded.

My task would be much more difficult if I had to assemble this whole idea from basic elements. Simply put, for any propaganda to be effective as mass persuasion, it must somehow resonate with ideas that are already in people's heads. To do otherwise is to attempt an entirely new installation of ideas and concepts, which requires far too much work on your part. So I have done the work for you, a sort of cognitive pre-packaging that takes advantage of the human propensity for efficiently avoiding work.

But don't mistake propaganda for a mere set of tricks. Nor am I trying to propagandize you at the moment, just trying to demonstrate a technique that I hope will draw your interest. I am acting within my role as a professor who has been intensely interested in propaganda for many years, and while professors (and writers) have quite often been propagandists for various causes, good and evil, wittingly and unwittingly, what I attempt here is merely to share a set of principles codified in the course of teaching and research. I do here what professors are supposed to do in an ideal world, which is to profess what they believe to be true and useful based on judgment, experience (real world and academic) and familiarity with a wide and deep body of well-vetted work that has been produced on their topic of specialization.

One might say this is education—beware, though, because education has, as often as not, conveyed a great deal of propaganda, and highly educated people tend to be more, not less, susceptible to propaganda than are the uneducated.[i] However, I prefer to think of my effort here as a continuation of a conversation that has been ongoing for many years in western culture. You may at some point wish to participate in this conversation. Also, more pragmatically, you may quite likely find this book useful for both offense and defense in your personal and professional life. You may imagine yourself unaffected by propaganda, but the person who thinks himself above propaganda is quite possibly its creature.[ii]

So here is my method. Although propaganda is an immense modern undertaking, I have tried to keep the text sparse and readable. After this introduction, in which I will attempt a synopsis of propaganda's arrival on the modern scene, I will move right on to the Commandments. Commentary, references and those "illuminating" digressions to which academics are prone are consigned to endnotes, some of which are self-contained essays in their own right.

A Match Made In Heaven

The purpose here is to promote readability without sacrificing depth or technical correctness. The endnotes will not only direct interested readers to other sources, but will show the interconnectedness of propaganda with social and administrative sciences and with other fields; for there is no getting away from propaganda. Any preaching on my part will be also confined to endnotes. The endnotes also summarize and comment on significant books, research papers, and their authors, including a few classic propaganda films (which I encourage you to watch online so as to better understand these "timeless" principles.)

The endnotes themselves provide a fairly good overview of history, research, and techniques of propaganda—especially within propaganda's social-scientific sister disciplines; for a great deal of social science, theory and method, especially social psychology, has been linked quite directly with improving or discovering mechanisms of propaganda. For example, survey research, now a universal practice, was essentially brought into widespread service in order to measure susceptibilities and effects of propaganda on target populations.[iii]

Each Commandment has its own chapter, although each can be applied in many ways, as befits general principles. The Commandments are simple, but have ramifying applications that will be suggested via straightforward examples. This may sometimes lead to a bit of overlap between the Commandments in their applications, but each Commandment as an action-principle remains nonetheless distinct. I will often employ extreme examples because they more clearly illustrate principles.

Just as it is in nowise the first, this book cannot in any sense be the last word on propaganda. This field of endeavor is too big, too specialized, too pressing, too ongoing for such a book to even exist. Propaganda has become one of the grand undertakings of modernity. Without it there could be no bureaucratic-corporate organizations or states, mass democratic or otherwise, for just as humans are characterized by an ability to communicate with each other, modern bureaucratic administrative organizations are characterized by a reliance on propaganda, both externally and the internally. Propaganda is a chief means by which the organizations that dominate modern life try to communicate power.[iv]

Propaganda as a Situation.

More than a mere set of techniques, propaganda is situational in nature. It is an organized bid for the right to interpret meaning in a given set of circumstances. The really big propagandas seek interpretive monopoly over the things that matter most. They are totalitarian in scope, e.g., religion, mass politics and social movements often seek to impose interpretations on the meaning of human existence, including its history, future, social relations, property, in short, aiming at the regulation of life itself.

Propagandas also occur on a much smaller scale as everyday attempts to monopolize or control meaning in local, more claustrophobic situations where there exist domains and resources worth contesting, e.g., school district or college administrators who serve out highly selective interpretations of reality so as to reinforce power, position and authority. Hence, propaganda scholar Jacques Ellul's wonderful remark that everything is explained thanks to propaganda.[v]

The benefits of these explanations, however, mostly accrue to their makers. Many definitions of propaganda have been put forward.[vi] Some are dramatic, some banal, some arcane, some narrow (there are many subtypes and techniques), and a few, downright obtuse. One of the more useful belongs to Walter Lippmann, who as a staffer in the Woodrow Wilson presidential administration saw firsthand the advent of modern American propaganda in the First World War.

A Match Made In Heaven
Lippmann viewed propaganda as inevitable in today's mass democracies, where voters are far removed physically and perceptually from political events, and must therefore rely on interpretive experts to inform their citizenship. We call it propaganda, said Lippmann, when a group of people who control access to some event releases information about it in such a way as to benefit themselves.[vii] Notice this implies both organization and self-interested interpretation of the meaning of reality.

A common misperception is that propaganda makers are necessarily the creatures of an ideology, culture or belief system, and their propaganda is primarily intended as a vehicle to disseminate these beliefs. While this is sometimes true, the situational view of propaganda suggests otherwise: in general, propaganda-making elites say and do what needs to be said and done to advance or maintain themselves and their organization. That they may also convince themselves with their own propaganda is beside the point. Their ideologies, as well as their actions, tend to be dictated by pragmatism and a will for power.

While many people may see this pseudomorphic tendency as a character defect,[viii] it accounts for the legendary slipperiness of politicians and bureaucrats, it may also be their chief survival skill. Propaganda's antecedent, persuasion, dates to before Aristotle's time, back when it was known simply as rhetoric. However, in modern times, the idea of rhetoric, which Aristotle formulated as an ethical and logical tool for arriving at truth through reasoned debate in face-to-face settings, has degenerated, more or less, into merely a set of tricks used to inform advertising and mass and organizational propagandas.[ix] "Rhetoric" accordingly has acquired negative connotations as the term is used in everyday speech,[x] while mass persuasion is merely a euphemism for propaganda.

I complete this introduction with a brief comprehensive history of propaganda. As a professor, I regard such a foundation as useful in obtaining a complete understanding. But the reader of material for practical application may well think otherwise and may wish to move directly on to the Commandments. You are in command.

Three Waves of Propaganda.

Propaganda can be thought of as having arrived in a progressive series of waves, each surging higher than the last. From its beginning, it has been the intimate companion of bureaucracy.

The First Wave

The first wave originates in the early 17th century when Pope Gregory XV established the Congregatio de Propaganda Fide, the congregation for the propagation of the faith, as an official department or ministry of the Roman Catholic Church. The Congregation was undoubtedly the first global communication/propaganda campaign and became, over time, so powerful that the cardinal in charge came to be called the Red Pope. Its scope included just about everything that had to do with propagation of organizational growth and uniformity of thought under Catholicism, in the Old and the New World, including establishment of national colleges for the education of priests, and missions to foreign nations.[xi]

Owing to this ecclesiastical origin, it was not until perhaps **100** years ago that the term propaganda crept into everyday language in the sense used today to connote informational manipulation in mass secular politics. Had someone been called a "propagandist" back in the 17th or 18th Century, however, it very likely would have been taken as a reference to a Jesuit priest. Propaganda was created in large part as a weapon against heretics, unbelievers and reformers as personified in Martin Luther and others, who had successfully challenged the interpretive monopoly that the Church had

A Match Made In Heaven

maintained for centuries regarding the meaning and conduct of life in Western Europe.

This monopoly had not been confined to the "merely" spiritual. God ruled Heaven and Earth and the "one true Church" effectively controlled access to God by means of a policy that reserved scripture reading and its interpretation, as well as the retail dispensation of Divine Grace via the sacraments, to Church officials: an unauthorized interpretation was "heresy," punishable by death. The Church functioned as God's exclusive agent, so it said, and was willing to back up this claim by any means necessary. It tolerated no competition.

The Reformation amounted to a rejection of this monopoly and the ecclesiastical bureaucracy that ran it. Protestants won the right to interpret absolute reality as they deemed it to be represented in scripture, thereby cutting out these middlemen. Please do not be misled into thinking that I am trying to beat up religion. I merely describe an informational sociology that benefited an elite, well-organized group. This is the situation of propaganda, an entirely earthly phenomenon. By means of this first world ministry of propaganda the Church attempted to re-impose informational dominance in new and improved form, i.e., it sought global uniformity of thought.

For an example of the spirit in which this effort was undertaken, Ignatius Loyola, founder of the Jesuits—the shock troops of this campaign—wrote: "To arrive at the truth in all things, we ought always to be ready to believe that what seems to us white is black, if the hierarchal Church so defines it." The Congregation of Propaganda was very successful, which explains, for instance, why much of the New World became and remains Catholic. But the Church never regained control over Northern Europe's Protestants or the Enlightenment Age philosophers —who went on to set up or influence new informational sociologies (some of which eventually amalgamated to become the United States of America).

Truth & Freedom

It is no coincidence that the origin of propaganda is coupled to another concept that defines the modern era—bureaucracy. When sociologist Max Weber described the emergence and characteristics of the rational scientific organization called bureaucracy, he used the Roman Catholic Church as a model. The Congregation of Propaganda was itself a model bureaucracy, with its many departments, protocols, reporting channels and national branches. So in these two vital areas—propaganda and bureaucracy—the Church's stamp upon modern secular life may prove even more enduringly pervasive than its spiritual one.

The Second Wave.

A second wave coincides with the First World War and its immediate aftermath. Talent, knowledge, new forms of mass media, communication technologies, governmental bureaucracy, need and circumstance all converged to establish a set of enduring practices. Viewed from the U.S. perspective, beginning in **1914**, British propagandists first directed their considerable ingenuity toward dragging America into the war. They used publicity techniques and social influence directed at American opinion leaders to inundate the U.S. with atrocity stories and accounts sympathetic to the brave Allies and helpless Belgium, across which the Germans had tromped. Belgium was sometimes portrayed as a maiden violated by a Kaiser-like gorilla, identifiable by a Prussian military uniform with its ridiculously pointed *pickelhaube* helmet (propaganda technique has relied much on heavy-handed stereotypes of this sort).

The British achieved a brilliantly simple mastery of the American informational sociology. Early on in the war, the British Navy cut the transatlantic cable from Germany, assuring henceforth that the great majority of war news going to America originated in Britain.[xii] The modern, popular use of the term propaganda as a pejorative and synonym for deceptive

A Match Made In Heaven

communication emerges about this time, but British and, later, American propagandists firmly linked its use with the Germans.

Upon entering the war officially in **1917** (it had already been supplying Britain with food, materials and munitions) America established an organization that set the pattern for professional propagandists ever since: the Committee on Public Information. CPI has been called "America's first propaganda ministry."[xiii]

CPI created massive public support for the war effort, despite a strong American isolationist tradition to stay out of "entangling" European alliances and wars. CPI quickly achieved near total interpretive dominance regarding the meaning of the War for Americans. In addition to providing newspapers with wholesome, staged photographs of the "boys" conscripted into military service and regular pre-written news articles on the war effort (nowadays called press releases), terms like morale, public opinion and, of course, public information were used to describe CPI's activities.

Total war begat total propaganda. Or perhaps it was the other way around—for total propaganda made total war into a moral obligation—i.e., it is one thing to conduct a limited war for strategic purposes, e.g., oil, and quite another to battle on behalf of Christian civilization. Few if any photographs of the four-million-plus military dead on the Allies' side ever appeared in any American or British newspaper.[xiv] This too was no accident. The war was so bloody and industrialized that some military professionals referred to the front lines as the "sausage factory"—fresh, identifiable cuts of meat in, sausage out.[xv]

The propagandists, however, focused on the glory and chivalric righteousness of the struggle. In America, while CPI's energetic director, George Creel, publicly eschewed censorship, CPI was distributing voluntary media guidelines that had more moral force than any mere government decree. CPI's **75,000** "four minute men," all civilian volunteers, spoke at local theaters on the talking points of the week, addressing a cumulative audience of more than 300 million individuals in the course of the war. Creel mobilized dramatists, college professors and students, authors, advertising professionals, film makers and artists—e.g., Charles Dana Gibson, creator of the "Gibson Girl," and a CPI Division of Pictorial Publicity produced posters, an important mass medium in that pre-television age.

Many perhaps seem corny by today's standards, e.g., "The United States Army Builds Men," which highlighted the crafts, character (depicted by a mail-clad knight) and physique that one could acquire by signing up. But much the same bait informs today's television recruiting ads, albeit upgraded by modern cinematographic technique. Creel underscored the importance the "battle of the fences," upon which the posters were hung. CPI was so successful that things German became anathema for a time in America—including German philosophy, music, surnames and the language itself. Picking up on themes in British propaganda, the Germans were characterized as murderers, nun-rapists and killers of babies— an atrocity attributed to the Germans was the game of bayonet catch played with babies.[xvi] Possibly, the only really clear and enduring outcome of that "war to end all wars" was to lodge the idea of propaganda into the American consciousness.

Later the American propagandists bragged, however, and it became quite apparent the Germans had not been the only propagandists, nor in fact had they been even particularly good propagandists. Creel published on how CPI "advertised" the war—a euphemism he evidently preferred over "propaganda." He rationalized CPI's manifold activities as the "battle for men's minds" and the "gospel of Americanism," which was spread not only within America, to both foreign and native-born via appropriate media and social channels, but also in Europe, Russia and Asia by means of American "news services."

When Congress curtailed CPI activities at war's end, former CPI functionaries began to apply their propagandistic skills on

A Match Made In Heaven

behalf of commercial interests. Thus was born the "industry" of public relations. Ed Bernays, a vivid example and regarded now as an iconic figure, appears to have invented the term public relations and taught the first university class on the subject. Using the terms propaganda and public relations interchangeably, he excelled at making "news" that furthered his employers' interests. He coined phrases such as "the engineering of consent" to describe this new science. [xvii]Also in this period was launched the academic-scientific study of propaganda.

At University of Chicago, Harold Lasswell wrote a seminal dissertation on propaganda technique in the World War, a field of endeavor that was eventually repackaged into the study of communication. Lippmann, progressing from propagandist to social commentator, published his famous Public Opinion, in which he pondered the problem of how to protect citizens from the mass opinion manufacturers. Concepts such as attitudes, public opinion, psychology and stereotypes were popularized. By the early 1920s Adolf Hitler was codifying his observations on military and mass movement propagandas that constitute perhaps the only sensible chapters in Mein Kampf.[xviii]

Lest the reader begin to think that I am merely stirring through the historical dust, all of these lines of inquiry remain sharply relevant today. For example, Lasswell's recipe, "How the enemy is to be treated in time of war," describes recent U.S. government information strategies in the Gulf War and the Iraq War to the point of being uncanny.[xix] Hitler, in turn, extolled (although by no means invented) the principles of simplicity and repetition that underlie much of modern mass consumerism and advertising.

Synthetic news techniques of the sort pioneered by Bernays and others now create most of the daily U.S. news stream; and although today's political communication scholars refer to these deceits as pseudo-events, they are real enough in their own way because they provide the only representations of political reality that most people will ever know.[xx] In these ways and others, bureaucratically-generated interpretations of reality overshadow virtually all other forms of social growth—e.g., in education, government and policy, and are announced and disseminated virtually in an ecclesiastical, top-down fashion.

In any case, by the 1920s it became obvious to many that wartime propaganda had poisoned the informational well of American rational democracy. Indignation over this continued until the World War II era. A prophylaxis attempted in the 1930s was the Institute for Propaganda Analysis, which among other activities, taught courses on propaganda in more than 500 American high schools.

IPA's touchingly naïve "ABC's of Propaganda" and "Seven Devices of Propaganda" were intended to protect innocents against the evils of special interest communications. The "devices" included glittering generalities, e.g., use of virtue words such as "justice" and "freedom" without any clear definition or meaning, and card-stacking, to indicate tendentiously manipulated arguments building toward a foregone conclusion.

The Third Wave.

The general mobilization of U.S. society in World War II signaled the end of such well-intentioned muddling. A whole generation of social scientists, often with government sponsorship, began to conduct research on how to do better, more effective propaganda. Some of the many areas explored included message design, credibility factors, inoculation against enemy propaganda, communication campaigns, communication effects from the manipulation of different variables, authority/obedience, content analysis (a way of quantifying communication content so trends and sources can be identified and propaganda measured) and the use of small groups (e.g., group dynamics) to change attitudes, and,

A Match Made In Heaven

especially, behaviors, through the means of normative group pressure.

This latter so-called "horizontal propaganda" conducted by means of the small group has since become the trend in social and corporate management practice; it tightens controls over employees while creating the illusion of democracy, a very advanced technique. Today there is more social science of this sort being taught in modern business schools than in university social science departments, so one might well wonder if U.S. society ever truly demobilized after the Second World War, when propaganda emerged as its social norm.

The Third Wave also produced or inspired volumes of social scientific research with direct applications to propaganda, inaugurating a golden age of behavioral studies that lasted until the 1960s or so. Perhaps the most memorable was Stanley Milgram's series of obedience to authority experiments. Milgram showed that under the guise of a "learning experiment," approximately 50 percent of workaday, average people would repeatedly administer 450-volt electric shocks to a restrained person.

They would continue despite screams and demands for release, and even after the restrained person became non-responsive and quite possibly dead or unconscious. Although the experiment was rigged, no shocks were actually delivered, screams pre-recorded, and the person supposedly being "shocked" was a confederate of the experimenters, the naïve subject who was giving the shocks did not know any of this. In effect, so I believe, Milgram synthesized the basic elements of mass murder/genocide in the laboratory—Nazified monsters were not necessarily an ingredient, just average people under a compelling set of circumstances.[xxi]

Truth & Freedom
Ubiquity of Propaganda.

Consider your own situation and behavior. Unless you happen to be reading this in a maximum-security prison, probably no armed guards oversee your activities. Instead you largely manage your own behavior based on ideas and expectations that have somehow found their way into your head. Education, training, socialization, information availability, habit and perception channel your actions in fairly predictable and productive ways, as far as the larger society is concerned. You are harnessed to something bigger than yourself. You quite possibly even imagine that you understand the larger world around you; which is perhaps a surer sign than any that some species of propaganda has taken hold.

Propaganda permeates modern mass-society democracy, which is based on nominal consent of the governed, and wherein coercion generally stands a safe remove in the background. Propaganda coordinates and connects mass democracy's human particles, assuring that many of them resonate on shared frequencies. Ellul believed that modern mass-man or woman needs propaganda as a matter of personal adjustment, necessary because of the relative meaninglessness of the individual in relationship to the mass.

Propaganda answers questions of greater meaning that were once the province of religion, myth, tradition and organic community.[xxii] It orients, assures and even provides an identity without having to go through all the work of building one's own. We have grown accustomed to its constant streaming—words-without-end-amen—much like listening to the radio or television provides an illusion of connection to the larger world when one is alone.

It wasn't always like this. Once upon a time propaganda was the exception. When Congress abruptly curtailed CPI activities at war's end in **1919**, it left many wartime matters hanging unexplained in America, e.g., President Wilson's peace treaty.

A Match Made In Heaven

Creel, however, who had propagandized on a scale unprecedented, accepted the cessation of official propaganda without any apparent reservation. Creel wrote:

Nothing would have been more instantly attacked, and justly attacked, than the use of governmental machinery and public funds for any such purpose. Bad as conditions are today, they would be infinitely worse had the President attempted to support his cause by "press-agenting" with the people's money. As for the Committee on Public Information, its duties ceased automatically when fighting ceased (401).

So the man who bragged of directing the global distribution of more than 75 million pieces of print propaganda, according to CPI records, had moral reservations about the use of propaganda in peacetime by elected democratic representatives who would unethically benefit by it.

How things have changed! Not only do few people nowadays express any such reservations, it would appear that yet fewer even conceive that such reservations might be in order. Today the White House alone employs several hundred propagandists or technicians in propaganda, in war and peace, at horrifying public expense, "press-agenting" with the people's money every day of the year. None of these support people are called propagandists, however.

I worked once on a presidential visit as an official of the host state. A White House representative and I did a walk-through of the prepared site. Behind the stage holding the bulletproof podium and the presidential seal, White House Communications personnel had set up a covered platform in an evergreen tree from which a technician would be operating the teleprompter. The representative lifted the canvas cover and said, "It's just like the Wizard of Oz: you pull back the curtain and there's a little guy operating the levers."

Truth & Freedom

We have become inured. I have often felt while trying to convey somewhat the scale of contemporary propaganda to today's mass media-bred students, that the task might be comparable to trying to explain the existence of water to a fish, a substance which constantly surrounds it, but of which it would quite likely be insensible. Much of what they seem to think they know about the world—fashion, music, current events, history—are but remnants of various propaganda/communication campaigns.

Not only has the public sector been long given over to the propagandists, so has much of the private corporate sector.[xxiii] Managerial elites use stockholder money, and, lately, public funds called bailouts and stimulus packages, to further the dodging of blame and taking of credit that sometimes seems to comprise their primary substantive expertise. Despite the ostensible business of these organizations, a main product seems to have transmogrified over time into propaganda, a process which organizational behaviorists call "goal displacement."[xxiv]

Corporate elites dominate the flow of information about their organizations in ways so as to confound even the most diligent inquiry. What stockholder or deadline-driven journalist has the time, energy and resources to conduct an independent investigation of a large, complicated corporate entity, private or public? Where even to begin? Informationally, the game always heavily favors insiders with direct access to events. British Prime Minister Lloyd George once said of the British War Department, which he had overseen in **1915-1918**, "They kept three sets of figures: one to mislead the public, another to mislead the government, and a third to mislead themselves."[xxv]

The more complicated things become, the more difficult they are to explain, yet there is more need than ever for explanation, and accordingly more opportunities arise for propaganda's handy explanations. Plus propaganda is much

A Match Made In Heaven

like an arms race—those who don't do it put themselves at a disadvantage, so the pressure is always to escalate.

Truth, Untruth, Propagandists and the Public Good.

Regarding the matter of truth, despite what has been said about atrocity stories, propaganda is not merely lies—although lies, rumors and disinformation have been used. But the lie is not a generally effective technique, despite the Nazi's famous notion about the "Big Lie" inspiring more belief than a small one. Overt lies, when detected, compromise the credibility of the propagandist; however, the propagandist can always use a front organization or "leaks" to outsource incredible claims while still preserving the appearance of probity.

Thus Ellul noted, in propaganda truth pays. There is no need to risk the lie when copious information consisting of select facts, arbitrary, operational definitions and statistics create a cognitive deluge which overwhelms the victim, who becomes therefore even more dependent on interpretive expert-propagandists to explain what it all means.

Additionally many matters within the province of propaganda are beyond truth or untruth per se, e.g., images or symbols. How can a photograph or an image be untrue? Unless offered as doctored evidence, an image merely is what it is. It may evoke a response, or a response to it can be conditioned through repetition, or it can be "interpreted," hence, in part, its power, e.g. the golden arches, the hammer and sickle.

This observation applies to slogans as well, which are often intentionally ambiguous so as to allow people to see in them whatever they need to see, e.g., "Change you can believe in," which means anything, everything or nothing depending on the perceiver's predispositions. Additionally, since the main thrust of propaganda has to do with the interpretation of meaning, which more often than not is ultimately unknown or in dispute, especially concerning complicated social issues, who is to say what may be the "correct" meaning of any major part of the human experience? The propagandist steps into this void, presenting a plausible case, perhaps one based on the crudest circumstantial evidence, but one suitable for his audience and purposes.

Who are all these propagandists? There is a powerful stereotype of the cartoon propagandist. Many still associate propaganda with Hitler, a residual effect that attests to the power of the American and British propaganda machinery in the Second World War.

Joseph Goebbels, Hitler's "minister of propaganda" was shown as a sort of crippled ridiculous dwarf (although no one was talking about FDR creaking about in his wheelchair). Propaganda was linked with the creation of Nazi automatons on a jackbooted and trench-coated goosestep through history.[xxvi] The propagandist-as-buffoonery stereotype was resurrected in the Iraq War in the person of Baghdad Bob, a virtual auto-parody, whom Americans loved to ridicule when CNN carried his out-of-skew reports on the progress of the war.

It also rode again in the "great-man" grotesqueries, the statues and monuments, of the Saddam Hussein regime. One might recollect the much-televised event when sundry persons identified as the Iraqi people pulled down the colossus of Hussein with much not-so-obtrusive help from the US military. The same trick had been pulled off in the film October, which commemorated the tenth anniversary of the 1917 Bolshevik Revolution in Russia, where "the people" are shown pulling down a colossus representing the Czar. Such demonstrations downplay the effectiveness of propaganda.

Rather than the monsters and their stooges, which are convenient to have around, on the whole propagandists are more or less low key; they prefer business attire to leather trench-coats, and are embedded in their organizations as bureaucrats and administrators, mundane in appearance and

A Match Made In Heaven

operation. Titles under which they operate are legion: vice president of external relations, lobbyists, government relations, public information specialists, communication directors, media specialists, publicity, any number of variants on "public relations"[xxvii] and whatever else circumstance may suggest. In **1913**, the US Congress designed a measure to ban use of publicity experts by U. S. government agencies, regarding this practice as unethical, and barred designated budget money for such use.

The gross result was merely that job titles changed. No one now has any firm idea just how many propaganda functionaries work for government—federal, state or local—partly because many have such nebulous job titles. Executives, for example, use their powers to attach such functionaries to budgets of departments that would seem to have nothing to do with propaganda, e.g., a Midwestern governor hires a person whom some would call a "political handler" with high level experience in a large national trade association, and situates him in the state's department of natural resources, where his only apparent function is to promote the governor.

Is propaganda evil by definition, or does it convey social benefits? It has often been defended or minimized. Lasswell discounted its long-term influence by claiming America's various propagandas would cancel each other out in a free marketplace of competing propagandas. This of course assumes a free market. Lasswell's assumption possibly no longer holds in the face of modern interpretive near-monopolies, e.g., government and ownership centralization, or the "cornering the market" in key areas within the information sociology, e.g., education policy, or the decline of citizen-based voluntary associations that might act as alternate information sources, and the concordant proliferation of staff-run groups wherein small, top-down organizations claim to speak on behalf of all humanity.

Bernays boasted that propaganda had helped to make America great by promulgating new products, markets and ideas. Others say that good propaganda works for the "public interest" while bad propaganda advances "special interests." Beware this line of argument, however, because autocrats routinely, if not invariably, claim the collective good as their warrant of personal legitimation.

Further, "special interests" may well be you or anyone else who doesn't go along with a current administrative agenda. Another common argument is that having more available information gives people more choices, so propagandists are therefore just providing a public service. Maybe this is true, but when information is thus subsidized it tends to serve those who have subsidized it, as is the case with press releases and think tank reports. Plus, propaganda is not neatly distinguishable from information.

Is there even such a thing as neutral information? For information doesn't just spontaneously appear in media—it serves some purpose. In any case, the lone individual is not up to the task of collecting raw data on world, national or even local events, and must depend on propaganda's interpretive experts to turn such data into information.

Some degree of propaganda may be good when viewed as a cost-benefit calculation, although we must always wonder who is doing the arithmetic. We might consider here the near universal belief among Americans of belonging to something called "the middle class," a pretense that is absurd on its face. If the belief is regarded as a socialization propaganda, however, which causes people to aspire and behave "correctly" according to cultural models, the belief assures that much unpleasant work continues to get done. Arguing the contrary, though, such a belief may have permanently injured many who don't know the difference between being a consumer and a citizen, and who haven't truly developed themselves because they imagine themselves as having already "arrived." It may also have

A Match Made In Heaven

damaged the nation by decreasing sustainable productivity and creating a false bubble of prosperity that appears recently to have burst.

Also, without propaganda societal unity might disappear. Extreme fragmentation might result. This was a fear of the Church as well, that without centralized control of meaning, the virtues of a higher, greater order might disappear and interpretive pluralism might degrade to the level where everyone merely strives against everyone else in a brutish Hobbesian fashion. Good or bad, however, propaganda is an omnipresent environmental fact. It seems impossible to imagine a mass society without it.

Is a Fourth Wave swelling over us now? Perhaps. It may be too early to say whether computer-mediated communications will be a boon to propagandists or, instead, to individual freedom. That people have more information than ever before may simply mean that they receive more highly customized propaganda. Or it could mean that online interpretive communities will be enabled, allowing people more independence in constructing social meaning. My own belief is that the Web is a godsend for propagandists as well as for autonomous interpretive communities; but with what long-term results I do not know.

Before commencing with the Commandments, let me add just this. Although informed by science, propaganda is an art. There are no magic buttons. Good. Were this so, human freedom would disappear. But even though no magic buttons may exist, there are many buttons to push, many techniques designed to push them and many functionaries devoted to the pushing of buttons.

Propaganda draws upon a great body of empirical knowledge. The Commandments incorporate this knowledge. Still, pragmatism drives the making of propaganda, as do the apparently unchanging needs of the human animal, an animal that is both rational and primitively emotional.

Propaganda adapts. It may be the closest thing available to a universal social lubricant; it has the additional advantage of being both recyclable and cheap to manufacture. You will find your own applications for this knowledge. But above all do not imagine yourself immune either from propaganda's effects, or if you work in a modern organization, from its necessity. Like any list of precepts, these commandments can serve either as a positive or a negative guide to behavior.

Patrick, Brian Anse (2011-10-07). The Ten Commandments of Propaganda Copyright 2011 Reproduced here with the kind permission of the author, Dr. Brian Anse Patrick, and Arktos Media Ltd, publishers of the print version of his book.

The book is available from Amazon:
http://amzn.com/B005TUDPHG - Kindle, and
http://amzn.com/1907166815 - Paperback.

A Match Made In Heaven
APPENDIX II.

Fifty Two Named Propaganda Techniques

Following is a list of 52 named techniques propagandist use to promote their messages, extracted and moderately edited from the article at **http://en.wikipedia.org/wiki/Propaganda**. The article is a somewhat brief overview of the history and practice of propaganda. The serious truth seeker can learn much by reading it.

1. **Ad hominem** - A Latin phrase that has come to mean attacking one's opponent, as opposed to attacking their arguments.

2. **Ad nauseam** - This argument approach uses tireless repetition of an idea. An idea, especially a simple slogan, that is repeated enough times, may begin to be taken as the truth. This approach works best when media sources are limited or controlled by the propagator

3. **Appeal to authority** - Appeals to authority cite prominent figures to support a position, idea, argument, or course of action.

4. **Appeal to fear** - Appeals to fear and seeks to build support by instilling anxieties and panic in the general population.

5. **Appeal to prejudice** - Using loaded or emotive terms to attach value or moral goodness to believing the proposition.

6. **Bandwagon** - Bandwagon and "inevitable-victory" appeals attempt to persuade the target audience to join in and take the course of action that "everyone else is taking".

7. **Inevitable victory** - Invites those not already on the bandwagon to join those already on the road to certain victory.

8. Join the crowd - This technique reinforces people's natural desire to be on the winning side. This technique is used to convince the audience that a program is an expression of an irresistible mass movement and that it is in their best interest to join.

9. Beautiful people - The type of propaganda that deals with famous people or depicts attractive, happy people. This makes other people think that if they buy a product or follow a certain ideology, they too will be happy or successful.

10. The Lie - The repeated articulation of a complex of events that justify subsequent action. The descriptions of these events have elements of truth, and the "big lie" generalizations merge and eventually supplant the public's accurate perception of the underlying events.

11. Black-and-white fallacy - Presenting only two choices, with the product or idea being propagated as the better choice. For example: "You're either with us, or against us...."

12. Classical conditioning - All vertebrates, including humans, respond to classical conditioning. That is, if object A is always present when object B is present and object B causes a negative physical reaction (e.g., disgust, displeasure) then when presented with object A when object B is not present, we will experience the same feelings.

13. Cognitive dissonance - People desire to be consistent. Suppose a pollster finds that a certain group of people hates his candidate for senator but loves actor A. They use actor A's endorsement of their candidate to change people" minds because people cannot tolerate inconsistency. They are forced to either to dislike the actor or like the candidate.

14. Common man – "The "plain folks" or "common man" approach attempts to convince the audience that the

A Match Made In Heaven

propagandist's positions reflect the common sense of the people.

15.   **Cult of personality** - A cult of personality arises when an individual uses mass media to create an idealized and heroic public image, often through unquestioning flattery and praise. The hero personality then advocates the positions that the propagandist desires to promote

16.   **Demonizing the enemy** - Making individuals from the opposing nation, from a different ethnic group, or those who support the opposing viewpoint appear to be subhuman (e.g., the Vietnam War-era term "gooks" for National Front for the Liberation of South Vietnam aka Vietcong, or "VC", soldiers), worthless, or immoral, through suggestion or false accusations.

17.   **Dictat**- This technique hopes to simplify the decision making process by using images and words to tell the audience exactly what actions to take, eliminating any other possible choices.

18.   **Disinformation** - The creation or deletion of information from public records, in the purpose of making a false record of an event or the actions of a person or organization, including outright forgery of photographs, motion pictures, broadcasts, and sound recordings as well as printed documents.

19.   **Door-in-the-face technique** - Is used to increase a person's latitude of acceptance. For example, if a salesperson wants to sell an item for $100 but the public is only willing to pay $50, the salesperson first offers the item at a higher price (e.g., $200) and subsequently reduces the price to $100 to make it seem like a good deal.

20.   **Euphoria** - The use of an event that generates euphoria or happiness, or using an appealing event to boost morale. Euphoria can be created by declaring a holiday, making luxury

items available, or mounting a military parade with marching bands and patriotic messages.

21. **Fear, uncertainty, and doubt** - An attempt to influence public perception by disseminating negative and dubious/false information designed to undermine the credibility of their beliefs

22. **Flag-waving** - An attempt to justify an action on the grounds that doing so will make one more patriotic, or in some way benefit a country, group or idea the targeted audience supports.

23. **Foot-in-the-door technique** - Often used by recruiters and salesmen. For example, a member of the opposite sex walks up to the victim and pins a flower or gives a small gift to the victim. The victim says thanks and now they have incurred a psychological debt to the perpetrator. The person eventually asks for a larger favor (e.g., a donation or to buy something far more expensive). The unwritten social contract between the victim and perpetrator causes the victim to feel obligated to reciprocate by agreeing to do the larger favor or buy the more expensive gift.

24. **Glittering generalities** - Glittering generalities are emotionally appealing words that are applied to a product or idea, but present no concrete argument or analysis. This technique has also been referred to as the PT Barnum effect.

25. **Half-truth** - A half-truth is a deceptive statement, which may come in several forms and includes some element of truth. The statement might be partly true, the statement may be totally true but only part of the whole truth, or it may utilize some deceptive element, such as improper punctuation, or double meaning, especially if the intent is to deceive, evade, blame or misrepresent the truth.

A Match Made In Heaven

26.   **Labeling** - A euphemism is used when the propagandist attempts to increase the perceived quality, credibility, or credence of a particular ideal. A Dysphemism is used when the intent of the propagandist is to discredit, diminish the perceived quality, or hurt the perceived righteousness of the Mark. By creating a "label" or "category" or "faction" of a population, it is much easier to make an example of these larger bodies, because they can uplift or defame the Mark without actually incurring legal-defamation.

27.   **Latitudes of acceptance** - If a person's message is outside the bounds of acceptance for an individual and group, most techniques will engender psychological reactance (simply hearing the argument will make the message even less acceptable). There are two techniques for increasing the bounds of acceptance. First, one can take a more even extreme position that will make more moderate positions seem more acceptable. This is similar to the Door-in-the-Face technique. Alternatively, one can moderate one's own position to the edge of the latitude of acceptance and then over time slowly move to the position that was previously.

28.   **Love bombing** - Used to recruit members to a cult or ideology by having a group of individuals cut off a person from their existing social support and replace it entirely with members of the group who deliberately bombard the person with affection in an attempt to isolate the person from their prior beliefs and value system

29.   **Lying and deception** - Lying and deception can be the basis of many propaganda techniques including Ad Homimen arguments, Big-Lie, Defamation, Door-in-the-Face, Half-truth, Name-calling or any other technique that is based on dishonesty or deception. For example, many politicians have been found to frequently stretch or break the truth

30.   **Managing the news** - According to Adolf Hitler "The most brilliant propagandist technique will yield no success

unless one fundamental principle is borne in mind constantly - it must confine itself to a few points and repeat them over and over." This idea is consistent with the principle of classical conditioning as well as the idea of "Staying on Message."

31.   **Milieu control** -An attempt to control the social environment and ideas through the use of social pressure

32.   **Name-calling** - Propagandists use the *name-calling technique* to incite fears and arouse prejudices in their hearers in the intent that the bad names will cause hearers to construct a negative opinion about a group or set of beliefs or ideas that the propagandist wants hearers to denounce. The method is intended to provoke conclusions about a matter apart from impartial examinations of facts. Name-calling is thus a substitute for rational, fact-based arguments against an idea or belief on its own merits.

33.   **Obfuscation**, - intentional vagueness, confusion Generalities are deliberately vague so that the audience may supply its own interpretations. The intention is to move the audience by use of undefined phrases, without analyzing their validity or attempting to determine their reasonableness or application. The intent is to cause people to draw their own interpretations rather than simply being presented with an explicit idea. In trying to "figure out" the propaganda, the audience forgoes judgment of the ideas presented. Their validity, reasonableness and application may still be considered.

34.   **Obtain disapproval** or *Reductio ad Hitlerum* - This technique is used to persuade a target audience to disapprove of an action or idea by suggesting that the idea is popular with groups hated, feared, or held in contempt by the target audience. Thus if a group that supports a certain policy is led to believe that undesirable, subversive, or contemptible people support the same policy, then the members of the group may decide to change their original position. This is a form of bad

logic, where a is said to include X, and b is said to include X, therefore, a = b.

35.   **Operant conditioning** - Operant conditioning involves learning through imitation. For example, watching an appealing person buy products or endorse positions teaches a person to buy the product or endorse the position. Operant conditioning is the underlying principle behind the Ad Nauseam, Slogan and other repetition public relations campaigns.

36.   **Oversimplification** - Favorable generalities are used to provide simple answers to complex social, political, economic, or military problems-

37.   **Pensée unique** - Enforced reduction of discussion by use of overly simplistic phrases or arguments (e.g., "There is no alternative to war."

38.   **Quotes out of context** - Selectively editing quotes to change meanings—political documentaries designed to discredit an opponent or an opposing political viewpoint often make use of this technique.

39.   **Rationalization (making excuses)** - Individuals or groups may use favorable generalities to rationalize questionable acts or beliefs. Vague and pleasant phrases are often used to justify such actions or beliefs.

40.   **Red herring** - Presenting data or issues that, while compelling, are irrelevant to the argument at hand, and then claiming that it validates the argument.

41.   **Repetition** - This is the repeating of a certain symbol or slogan so that the audience remembers it. This could be in the form of a jingle or an image placed on nearly everything in the picture/scene.

42. **Scapegoating** - Assigning blame to an individual or group, thus alleviating feelings of guilt from responsible parties and/or distracting attention from the need to fix the problem for which blame is being assigned.

43. **Slogans** - A slogan is a brief, striking phrase that may include labeling and stereotyping. Although slogans may be enlisted to support reasoned ideas, in practice they tend to act only as emotional appeals. Opponents of the US's invasion and occupation of Iraq use the slogan "blood for oil" to suggest that the invasion and its human losses was done to access Iraq's oil riches. On the other hand, supporters who argue that the US should continue to fight in Iraq use the slogan "cut and run" to suggest withdrawal is cowardly or weak.

44. **Stereotyping** -This technique attempts to arouse prejudices in an audience by labeling the object of the propaganda campaign as something the target audience fears, hates, loathes, or finds undesirable. For instance, reporting on a foreign country or social group may focus on the stereotypical traits that the reader expects, even though they are far from being representative of the whole country or group; such reporting often focuses on the **anecdotal.** In graphic propaganda, including war posters, this might include portraying enemies with stereotyped racial features.

45. **Straw man** - A straw man argument is an informal fallacy based on misrepresentation of an opponent's position. To "attack a straw man" is to create the illusion of having refuted a proposition by substituting a superficially similar proposition (the "straw man"), and refuting it, without ever having actually refuted the original position.

46. **Testimonial** - Testimonials are quotations, in or out of context, especially cited to support or reject a given policy, action, program, or personality. The reputation or the role (expert, respected public figure, etc.) of the individual giving the statement is exploited. The testimonial places the official

sanction of a respected person or authority on a propaganda message. This is done in an effort to cause the target audience to identify itself with the authority or to accept the authority's opinions and beliefs as its own.

47.   **Third party technique** Works on the principle that people are more willing to accept an argument from a seemingly independent source of information than from someone with a stake in the outcome. It is a marketing strategy commonly employed by Public Relations (PR) Firm that involves placing a premeditated message in the "mouth of the media." Third party technique can take many forms, ranging from the hiring of journalists to report the organization in a favorable light, to using scientists within the organization to present their perhaps prejudicial findings to the public. Frequently Astroturf groups or front groups are used to deliver the message.

48.   **Thought-terminating cliché** - A commonly used phrase, sometimes passing as folk wisdom, used to quell cognitive dissonance.

49.   **Transfer** - Also known as **association**, this is a technique that involves projecting the positive or negative qualities of one person, entity, object, or value onto another to make the second more acceptable or to discredit it. It evokes an emotional response, which stimulates the target to identify with recognized authorities. Often highly visual, this technique often utilizes symbols (e.g. swastikas) superimposed over other visual images (e.g. logos). These symbols may be used in place of words.

50.   **Selective truth** - Richard Crossman, the British Deputy Director of Psychological Warfare Division (PWD) for the Supreme Headquarters Allied Expeditionary Force (SHAEF) during the Second World War said "In propaganda truth pays. It is a complete delusion to think of the brilliant propagandist as being a professional liar. The brilliant propagandist is the

man who tells the truth, or that selection of the truth which is requisite for his purpose, and tells it in such a way that the recipient does not think he is receiving any propaganda. The art of propaganda is not telling lies, but rather selecting the truth you require and giving it mixed up with some truths the audience wants to hear."

51.   **Unstated assumption** - This technique is used when the idea the propagandist wants to plant would seem less credible if explicitly stated. The concept is instead repeatedly assumed or implied.

52.   **Virtue words** - These are words in the value system of the target audience that produce a positive image when attached to a person or issue. Peace, happiness, security, wise leadership, freedom, "The Truth", etc. are virtue words. Many see religiosity as a virtue, making associations to this quality affectively beneficial. Their use is considered of the *Transfer* propaganda technique

A Match Made In Heaven
APPENDIX III.

The Record of Chapter IV

Here are the nine steps:

1. Identify and record in detail the question you will answer or the problem you will solve. If you are attempting a sub-problem or question, record how it relates to the overall problem or question. Coming up with a useful result requires that you do this sub-question research; it will save a lot a wasted effort if you do the research up front.

2. Determine and summarize in writing the current status of previous and ongoing efforts to answer the question or solve the problem.

3. Record the data sources, initial assumptions and axioms that will guide the investigation. This is a crucial step, which if done carelessly or without sufficient thought, can lead one far astray.

4. Search a sub-set of the available information until you find enough information to suggest an answer to the question or solution to the problem. Record that answer as the initial working hypothesis. Summarize the reasons you think it may be the solution.

> **a.** No accumulation of supporting information can **prove** a hypothesis or assumption, but there must be **some** minimal amount of substantial supporting evidence for the conclusion to be credible. **For this process, the absolute minimum acceptable supporting evidence is determined by God's criterion – there must be at least two (substantial) "witnesses".**
>
> **b.** It is commonly accepted that a scientific hypothesis (or assumption) must be modified or rejected

altogether if even one substantial bit of contradictory information is found to exist. I will often be dealing with recorded information, not natural phenomena. Since records can become corrupted and made unreliable, I will adopt for my **Rejection Criterion: an assumption or hypothesis must be rejected if there exist at least two substantial bits of information that could not exist if the assumption or hypothesis were true.**

5. Continue exploring the information, looking for evidence that confirms or contradicts the working hypothesis. Record that information, and whether it is supporting or contradictory.

6. Modify the working hypothesis, if necessary, to accommodate any substantial contradictory evidence. Record modified hypotheses using appropriate identifiers, for example, by numbering them as you adopt them.

7. Repeat step 6 exploring information not yet considered until a substantial portion of the available information has yielded significant evidence confirming the latest working hypothesis while revealing no contradictory information. Record this as your answer to the question or solution to the problem.

8. Report in an appropriate medium the final hypothesis, verified by your research, as an answer worth believing to the question or solution of the problem.

9. Preserve the records of all this. You will need them later to answer questions about your conclusions or your methods.

By completing the process and reporting the results, you have established your position on that question or problem. The exploratory work is completed and now you must prepare to defend it against spurious attacks and amend it if a reasonable analysis shows it needs amending.

A Match Made In Heaven

The Record

Numbers refer to steps in the process

1. The Questions: Basic Question: Why did Christ die on the cross?

Questions to be answered first:

    a. Were there people enslaved to Satan at the time of the Crucifixion?

    b. Did Jesus give His life to free mankind from slavery or to transfer ownership of Satan's slaves to God?

2. Summary of current understanding:

Rather than create another summary, I will copy here an excerpt from an article produced by one from the orthodox perspective. There are many, many such articles to choose from. I have chosen this one for three reasons, it is reasonably brief, it covers most of the prominent theories of atonement, and it is free from the obvious bias exhibited by the authors of the other articles I have read. The author follows this piece by his proposal for an alternate Theory of Atonement. If you wish to explore that, you can find the article just by searching for it on Google, using its title.

[Begin Article]
Understanding Atonement: A New and Orthodox Theory

Robin Collins

Copyright 1995

(May be distributed and quoted if credit is properly given and it is noted that the work is still in progress.)

Suppose a theologian told the following parable:

Truth & Freedom

There was a man who had two sons. The younger said to his father, "Father, give me my share of the estate." So the father divided his property between them. Not long after that, the younger son went off to a distant country, squandered all he had in wild living, and ended up feeding pigs in order to survive. Eventually he returned to his father, saying, "Father, I have sinned against heaven and you. I am no longer worthy to be called your son. Make me one of your hired servants." But his father responded, "I cannot simply forgive you for what you have done, not even so much as to make you one of my hired men. You have insulted my honor by your wild living. Simply to forgive you would be to trivialize sin; it would be against the moral order of the entire universe. For nothing is less tolerable in the order of things than for a son to take away the honor due to his father and not make recompense for what he takes away. Such is the severity of my justice that reconciliation will not be made unless the penalty is utterly paid. My wrath--my avenging justice--must be placated."

"But father, please." the son began to plead.

"No," the father said, "either you must be punished or you must pay back, through hard labor for as long as you shall live, the honor you stole from me."

Then the elder brother spoke up. "Father, I will pay the debt that he owes and endure your just punishment for him. Let me work extra in the field on his behalf and thereby placate your wrath." And it came to pass that the elder brother took on the garb of a servant and labored hard year after year, often long into the night, on behalf of his younger brother. And finally, when the elder brother died of exhaustion, the father's wrath was placated against his younger son and they lived happily for the remainder of their days.[4]

A Match Made In Heaven

The above parable will strike many of you as a perverted version of Jesus' parable of the Prodigal Son. And, I believe, it should. Yet it essentially embodies the most widely accepted story of the Atonement that has been told in Western Christianity since the time of Anselm in the eleventh century, and as George Foley notes (232), has been the basis ever since the Protestant Reformation for what has been called Evangelical Theology. As we shall see, this story is actually a mixture of two theories of the Atonement--

Anselm's Debt or Satisfaction theory, and the Penal theory of the Reformers--theories which essentially say that Christ's death satisfied the debt demanded by the moral order, or paid the penalty demanded by divine justice, for our sins. Many Christians have read and heard these ideas countless times in books and sermons, and such teachings probably have seemed perfectly acceptable, sensible, and biblical.

We might ask, however: if these theories (which are closely related) are really quite unbiblical when their claims are transposed into the concrete situation of Jesus' parable, why have they been accepted by so many Christians? And are they really the only alternatives available?

Truth & Freedom
A Distinction between Doctrine and Theory

To begin answering these questions, we need to make a crucial distinction between the <u>doctrine</u> of the Atonement and a <u>theory</u> of the Atonement. The <u>doctrine of the Atonement</u> is essentially the claim that through Christ's life, death, and Resurrection, we are saved from sin and reconciled to God. A <u>theory</u> of the Atonement, on the other hand, is an explanation of both <u>how</u> and <u>why</u> Christ's life, death, and Resurrection was in some sense necessary to save us from sin and reconcile us to God.

Now, the <u>doctrine</u> of the Atonement is absolutely essential to the proclamation of the gospel and hence Christianity, for the gospel is just this proclamation that through Christ's life and death, and our faith in that event, we are saved from sin and reconciled to God. This is not so with <u>theories</u> of the Atonement, however. Not only have many theories of the Atonement been offered throughout Church history, but no theory of the Atonement has been considered a matter of Church dogma.

For example, no such theory is included in any of the formative creeds, nor was any such theory pronounced by any of the early authoritative councils which decided on the canon of scripture and the basic teachings of Christianity. Moreover, although scripture could plausibly be said to support some theories over others, nowhere in scripture is any particular theory actually stated. Thus, much room is left open to theorize concerning this central doctrine and yet remain both orthodox and true to scripture.

Below, I am going to argue that the Satisfaction and Penal theories of the Atonement are so unsatisfactory that we would be better off simply to accept the doctrine of the Atonement as a mystery than to accept one of

A Match Made In Heaven

them. I believe that so many people have accepted the dominant Western theories because of confusion about the difference between the doctrine of the Atonement and theories of the Atonement, because of tradition, and, probably most significantly, because of the lack of any better alternative theory. After critiquing the traditional Western theories, therefore, I shall develop, in a philosophically careful and clear way, a much more adequate theory. First, however, let's put all this theorizing in historical perspective.

A Brief History of Theories of the Atonement in the West

The first major theory of the Atonement to be put forth in Western Christianity was the Bargain or Ransom theory. Essentially, this theory claimed that Adam and Eve sold humanity over to the Devil at the time of the Fall; hence, justice required that God pay the Devil a ransom to free us from the Devil's clutches. God, however, tricked the Devil into accepting Christ's death as a ransom, for the Devil did not realize that Christ could not be held in the bonds of death. Once the Devil accepted Christ's death as a ransom, this theory concluded, justice was satisfied and God was able to free us from Satan's grip.

During the first formative centuries of Christianity this reasoning seemed plausible to many Christians, but it was never made a required belief. Although the Ransom theory dominated for the first thousand years of Western Christian thought on the subject, since the eleventh century it has been almost entirely abandoned by trained theologians largely because of what has been considered a devastating critique by Anselm, a major medieval philosopher and theologian. According to this critique, since the Devil is an outlaw himself, he could never have a just claim on us. Hence, Anselm argued, God did not need to pay the Devil anything to free us.[5] *Since it is generally agreed to this day that Anselm's critique dispatches this theory, there is no need to address or critique it further here.*

Along with critiquing the Ransom theory, Anselm systematically developed an alternative theory, what has come to be known as the Debt or Satisfaction theory, the second major Western theory of the Atonement. According to the Satisfaction theory we have contracted a debt of obligation to God because of our sin. God, however, could not simply forgive our debt. God's honor and the order of the universe, Anselm claimed, require that either we be punished or the debt be paid (satisfied). Since we could not pay ourselves, this theory goes, God the Son paid our debt for us by being perfectly obedient to God the Father, even to the point of suffering and dying on the Cross. Once this debt was satisfied, God was free to shower us with his mercy and thereby free us from sin and reconcile us to himself, given that we repent and respond to his grace.

At about the same time as Anselm, the theologian/philosopher Peter Abelard developed the third major western theory of the Atonement, which has become known as the Moral Exemplar theory. According to this theory, Christ's life and death save us by giving us a perfect moral example of love, humility, and obedience to follow. Many Christians over the centuries have found this idea spiritually edifying and helpful for practical discipleship. Others, however, have dismissed this theory as being inadequate to scripture, and I believe they are largely right, at least in the way this theory is commonly presented. The main problem with this idea (at least as a theory of Atonement) is that it implies that Jesus' life, death, and Resurrection do not play a significantly greater role in our salvation than that played by John the Baptist, Socrates, or Mother Teresa--

A Match Made In Heaven

each of whom in various ways provides a good, though not perfect, moral example for us to imitate or to draw inspiration from. In fact, based on this theory, one could argue that Jesus plays a significantly lesser role: since many contemporary examples are *more* like us in many important respects than Jesus Christ, who after all was unlike us in being morally perfect and living two thousand years ago, these other models should be easier to imitate and thus *more* effective than Jesus in inspiring us. But the New Testament implies that Jesus played a crucial role in our salvation, a role qualitatively different from that of anyone else. So, although Jesus certainly did provide an inspiring moral example and this basic idea has many merits, the Moral Exemplar theory does not by itself adequately account for the doctrine of the Atonement and hence I shall not consider it further here.[6]

The fourth major theory of the Atonement, the Penal Theory, was developed centuries after Anselm and Abelard by the Protestant Reformers and those who followed them. The Penal theory is actually an updated and modified version of the Satisfaction theory; instead of saying that Christ paid a debt we owed, it simply claims instead that Christ took the punishment we deserved. According to the Penal theory, justice, or the moral order, requires that our sin be punished. Christ, however, the theory claims, satisfied this demand of justice by enduring our punishment for us on the Cross, and thus opened the way for God's grace in our lives. Though historically the latest major theory to arrive on the scene, the Penal theory is probably the most widely known and influential interpretation of the doctrine of the Atonement in Western Christianity.

Since the time of the Protestant Reformation, almost all Western theories of the Atonement have been largely variations of Anselm's Satisfaction theory, the Penal theory, and the Moral Exemplar theory. All these theories we have discussed share one thing in common: they understand the basic relationship of God to the world primarily in terms of moral law, and the Satisfaction and Penal theories explicitly use judicial notions and the imagery of the courtroom. More conservative Christians, both Catholic and Protestant, typically adopt some variation or combination of the Satisfaction and Penal theories, and liberal Christians, both Protestant and Catholic, have commonly adopted some variation of the Moral Exemplar theory. Indeed, among many conservative circles, particularly Evangelical circles, the Satisfaction and Penal theories have become very deeply ingrained. For instance, Anselm's Satisfaction theory has become embodied in standard Christian hymns and songs with which most of us are familiar, such as the one which tells us that "He paid a debt He did not owe," and "I owed a debt I could not pay," (Grogan). Moreover, these theories are frequently preached from the pulpit as though they were identical with the gospel proclamation as found in scripture: how many times, for instance, have we heard the gospel accounts of Jesus' life, death and Resurrection explained as a story about how Christ paid our punishment and thereby satisfied the demands of divine justice (i.e. the Penal theory)? Yet, as many writers on the subject have noted, nowhere does scripture say these things; rather, they are fairly late interpretations of scripture, interpretations about which orthodox Christians have disagreed throughout the centuries, both in the East and West. For example, as the Church historian L. W. Grensted has pointed out, "Before the Reformation only a few hints of a Penal theory can be found. After the Reformation it became the common ground for a great majority of Protestant writers" *(191)*. All of this should convince us that the standard theories of the Atonement

A Match Made In Heaven

should not simply be accepted as part of standard Christian teaching. Rather, these theories must be judged on how well they provide a philosophically, ethically, theologically, and biblically sound explanation and understanding of the doctrine of the Atonement, something I will now argue that they fail to do.

A Brief Critique of the Satisfaction and Penal Theories

In this section I will not try to give a full scale critique of the Penal and Satisfaction theories, but will instead simply point to some major logical problems with each of these theories that should motivate us to consider the alternative theory I will later be proposing. The main problem with the Satisfaction and Penal theories involves their effectiveness <u>as theories</u>. If you really think about it, they never actually help us understand the doctrine of the Atonement, and thus they fail to accomplish what theories of the Atonement are designed to do--that is, help us make sense of the doctrine. To see this, note that in order for a theory to make any real progress in making sense of the Atonement it must not 'explain' the doctrine of the Atonement at the cost of making some <u>new</u> claims that are <u>at least as</u> puzzling as the doctrine itself.[7]

But this is exactly what these two theories do. They only eliminate our puzzlement regarding the doctrine of the Atonement by introducing two new claims that are at least as perplexing: namely, 1) the claim that God cannot simply forgive our sin but must demand repayment, even if we repent and deeply recognize the wrongness of our acts, and 2) the claim that the debt of obligation or punishment for our sin can be paid by another, namely Christ, and that this satisfies the demands of the moral order. It is especially difficult to see how this latter claim could be true, particularly once we take into account that according to orthodox

Truth & Freedom

Christian doctrine Christ is God, and hence one of the persons who we have sinned against, one of the "victims" of our crimes. If I were to stab you, neither justice nor the moral order would be satisfied by you, the victim, causing yourself further suffering by, for example, whipping or hanging yourself in order to pay the penalty for my crime.

In response to this logical problem, people commonly try to make sense of these theories by appealing to legal cases in which one person pays the debt of another, such as a parent paying her child's traffic ticket. This response, however, fails, for although this type of event commonly happens, the laws that allow it to happen, such as speeding laws, are not designed to institute the demands of justice, but rather to keep order in society (i.e., they are <u>civil</u> laws). Instead, the truly analogous legal cases are those in which we think that justice demands punishment, such as in murder cases (i.e. those involving <u>criminal</u> laws). But these are the very cases in which we do <u>not</u> think that justice is satisfied by someone else paying the criminal's penalty, such as a mother going to the electric chair in place of her son. In Anselm's time, however, even criminal offenses such as murder were handled like traffic tickets with the payment of money, because the concern of that society was not so much to ensure justice for the victim as to prevent violent retaliation by the victim's family, and the social chaos which would result from blood feuds of this sort. In the medieval legal system, therefore, not only could money substitute for punishment, but it didn't even matter who paid the money. This is why the notion that a third party could pay a criminal's debt of obligation, and that this could adequately substitute for a criminal punishment such as a death penalty, made some sense within Ansel's culture, but we now feel it doesn't really satisfy the demands of justice.

A Match Made In Heaven

*I conclude, therefore, that the Satisfaction and Penal theories do not help us make sense of the Atonement, but rather make it more puzzling than it was before. Lest I be misunderstood, it is important to stress at this point that I am **not** arguing that just because we can't understand how divine justice could be satisfied by Christ paying our supposed debt of obligation, these theories must be false. After all, I recognize that there are many truths about God and the world that are mysterious or difficult to understand from a human perspective, such as the doctrine of the Trinity.*

Rather, all I am claiming is that because the central claims of these two theories of the Atonement are <u>at least as</u> puzzling from a human perspective as the doctrine of the Atonement itself, they do not really make any progress in explaining or helping us to understand the Atonement, <u>and thus they fail to do what a theory of the Atonement is designed to do.</u> Therefore, unless we have other strong reasons to believe these theories, something I claim we don't have, we would be better off simply accepting the doctrine as a mystery than accepting one of these theories.

The above argument applies to both theories. When we look at the Satisfaction theory, however, even worse problems lurk in the shadows, particularly surrounding its claim that God cannot simply forgive our debt of sin without demanding repayment, as I might forgive a debt you owe me.

To see the problem clearly, first note that if we consider God the Son as one with God the Father, the Atonement under the Satisfaction view simply amounts to God paying God, which is equivalent to God forgiving the debt. On the other hand, if we consider God the Son as distinct from God the Father, the question arises: Who pays the debt we owe to God the Son because of our sin

against him? If Christ--that is, God the Son--pays it, that is equivalent to God the Son paying himself and hence forgiving it. But if God the Son can forgive the debt we owe him, why can't the Father do the same? So either way you look at it, it turns out that God the Father can simply forgive our debt without demanding repayment, contrary to the central claim of the Satisfaction theory.
End of Article

Step 3. Data Sources, Assumptions and Axioms:

a. The information source we will use is the Bible as we have it today. The Bible says it is the very word of God, and is said to contain all any person needs to know about who God is, what he is like, who and what man is, and what the relationship between God and man is to be. We will follow the example of the Orthodox Churches and choose the Greek New Testament and the Greek Septuagint Old Testament as our data sources.

b. We will choose the Septuagint for the same reasons the Orthodox Churches do – the Septuagint was translated before 250 BC, long before the rise of Christianity, by a group of scholars who spoke both Greek and Hebrew. The Masoretic Text, the other available alternative and used by all Protestants, was compiled over about five centuries before the 10th century AD. The Septuagint predates the first Masoretic Old Testament by over 1000 years. And, the Masoretic wording is alleged to have been deliberately altered to remove support for the Christian message. This assertion is supported to some extent by discoveries of discrepancies between that text and older texts in the Dead Sea Scrolls.

c. If God is who the Bible says He is, and if He has the powers and knowledge it says He has, we needn't question whether the Bible is what it says it is. The God described in the Bible is perfectly able to cause that book to be written,

A Match Made In Heaven

and perfectly able to preserve it from any attempt to destroy it or change its message. We can be confident we are doing the right thing in choosing the older Greek version; especially since it is much easier for us westerners to understand the Greek than the Hebrew.

Understand, please, we have decided to take the Bible as our information source (**an axiom**); we will not concern ourselves with questions about its reliability. The question is, "What does the Bible have to say about this issue?" If we do find a consistent, credible message in words written over thousands of years, that will lend credibility to the claim the Bible makes for itself – that it was written by God for the benefit of mankind. But that itself is not a question we will consider in this chapter or in this book.

Because we want to understand God's message to us, we won't concern ourselves with outside information. Translations are easily influenced by the mindset of the translators, so we ultimately will rely on the words of the original Greek. Not being skilled in reading Greek, we will use translations for our initial understanding and turn to the Greek for the precise meaning of important words.

I have long used for the basic meaning of words Strong's Exhaustive Concordance of the Bible and Thayer's Greek-English Lexicon of the New Testament. I have found new resources, **E-Sword (www.esword.org)**, a free bible application, and **www.biblelexicon.org,** an online tool, indispensible for this work.

"These things have been studied to death for a couple of thousand years," you should be thinking about now. "What makes you think you have any chance of coming up with truth that has been overlooked by everyone else?" That's a good question; here's the answer:

Truth & Freedom

The difference is in the approach. I'll take an approach the thinkers of 500 years ago couldn't take because the process hadn't been invented yet. We will tackle this body of information just like we would a problem in physics, say, or a crime scene investigation. Follow along and see how this works out.

The Acceptance Criteria you will use in deciding to retain or revise assumptions and hypotheses. These criteria, taken together, comprise the axiom that controls the process. Here are the Acceptance Criteria I will use in all that follows:

> d. No accumulation of supporting information can **prove** a hypothesis or assumption, but there must be **some minimal** amount of substantial supporting evidence for the conclusion to be credible. **For this process, the absolute minimum acceptable supporting evidence is determined by God's criterion – there must be at least two (substantial) "witnesses".**

It is commonly accepted that a scientific hypothesis (or assumption) must be modified or rejected altogether if even one substantial bit of contradictory information is found to exist. I will often be dealing with recorded information, not natural phenomena. Since records can become corrupted and made unreliable, I will adopt for my **Rejection Criterion: an assumption or hypothesis must be rejected if there exist at least two substantial bits of information that could not exist if the assumption or hypothesis were true.**

Here are my initial assumptions:

> a. There exists, and has existed forever, a spirit being, who created every physical, material thing that now exists, has existed and will exist. He created man in his own image (in some sense) with a specific purpose in mind. He has worked ever since to bring that purpose to fulfillment.

A Match Made In Heaven

b. He has caused to be written, and has preserved for us and those who follow us, a Book, the Bible, containing the information we need to know if we are to understand who He is, what His purpose for us is, and how we are to interact with Him and with His creation, including specifically our fellow man. Every word in that Book has meaning for someone, sometime, someplace, not necessarily for all men in all times and in all places.

c. The message from God to man communicated by the words of the Book is absolutely true and trustworthy, having from the beginning been protected by Him. Included in that message is what we are to know about God – His attributes: omnipotence, omnipresence, His perfect knowledge, love, righteousness, justice and truth.

d. These assumptions, and all supplementary assumptions, are subject to verification or falsification by evidence contained in the Book.

Step 4. Having identified our data set and listed our initial assumptions and axioms, we are ready to **form a working hypothesis** – a kind of trial theory – that promises to help us discover the answer we are looking for. Once we've recorded that hypothesis so we and others who critique our work can see what we've done, we will begin searching for evidence supporting or contradicting our hypothesis. Finding supporting evidence will encourage us to look further; finding contradictory evidence will mean that we will have to revise our hypothesis or abandon it altogether.

We form our working hypothesis after looking at some of the evidence in the New Testament. Here we see a young man, the son of a carpenter, embarking on a preaching ministry after being baptized by his cousin. We're struck by the fact that some of his teaching is in the form of parables.

Truth & Freedom

Why parables? Doesn't he want the people to understand what he's telling them? Why go to all that trouble just to leave people in the dark about what he's saying? Jesus said he spoke for the Father (John 14:10). If everything he said came from the Father, and if the Father intended the Bible to communicate a message to us, then he must have had a purpose for speaking in parables. Jesus answers this question in Matthews Gospel:

And the disciples came and said to Him, "Why do you speak to them in parables?" Jesus answered them, "To you it has been : granted to know the mysteries of the kingdom of heaven, but to them it has not been granted ... Therefore I speak to them in parables; (so that) (while) seeing they do not see, and (while) hearing they do not hear, nor do they understand." (Matt 13:10, 13 NASB, edited to show the Greek meanings.)

The translation uses *because* instead of *so that*; the Greek word has both meanings. The *seeing* and *hearing* are participles, and properly are translated *while seeing* and *while hearing*

Jesus' answer, as amended, tells us that Jesus taught in parables because God wanted **only His own people** to understand the message of the parable. That would make sense if He knew that rebellious men would distort His message if they understood it. His answer suggests that not all Bible messages are plainly stated, and suggests to us one way God used to preserve the scripture message.

Let's assume that was His purpose. **Let's include that in our working hypothesis – Jesus used parables in part to teach us that not all the Bible's messages, though communicated by the words of the text, are stated plainly and openly.**

Then we recall a conversation Jesus had with a group of Jews *who believed him,*

If you hold to my teaching, you are really my disciples. Then you will know the truth and the truth will set you free.

A Match Made In Heaven

They answered him, We are Abraham's descendants and have never been slaves to anyone. How can you say that we shall be set free?

Jesus replied, I tell you the truth, everyone who sins is a slave to sin. (John 8:31-34. (NIV)

Here's something interesting. What's this talk about being slaves and being set free? Everyone who sins, he said. Paul tells us all have sinned. (Rom 3:23) Taken together, **those two passages give us another part of our hypothesis – We all are – or have been – slaves – to sin – whatever that means.**

Moving on into Romans, we find a clear statement telling how one can become a slave. *Don't you know that when you offer yourselves to someone to obey him as slaves, you are slaves to the one you obey – whether you are slaves to sin, which leads to death, or to obedience, which leads to righteousness?* (Rom 6:16)

This verse seems to teach us that a person can become a slave simply by agreeing to obey someone.

Now we can write down the initial working hypothesis that will guide us as we begin to look for the message in the scriptures.

Our initial working hypothesis:

    a. **The Bible as we have received it, in the plain meaning of the Septuagint and the Greek New Testament, is the information source we'll use to discover God's message. We will not question its accuracy or probability of being true. That is a separate task. Our task is to find the message in the body of information presented to us.**

    b. **Using the process described in Chapter 3 will lead us to a credible message from the Bible.**

c. **Jesus used parables in part to teach us that not all the Bible's messages are stated plainly and openly, that sometimes the message communicated by the story is not stated in the words of the story.** (Finding messages not explicitly stated is nothing new in Bible study; we accept many truths that are not explicitly stated, the doctrine of the Trinity being one of them.)

d. **When we encounter material that appears to be a parable, we will look for the message God intends us to find in the parable.**

e. **We all are or have been slaves to something.** (Jesus said as much; it will pay us to keep that in mind as we progress.)

f. **A free man can become a slave just by agreeing to obey another**, accepting his lordship in exclusion of all others. We will take the warning in Rom **6:16** to be literally true.

Step 5. Armed with these ideas, this hypothesis, we'll look at the scriptures to try to understand the real situation in which mankind finds itself.

Here is what we have discovered:

a. **Israel/Jacob was the son of Isaac, the son of Abraham.**

b. **A slave is dependent upon his master for everything.**

c. God could truthfully call Jacob his (figurative) son if Isaac were His slave.

d. Isaac would have been born God's slave if Abraham was His slave. But in that case, God would have called Isaac his firstborn.

A Match Made In Heaven

e. Abraham told Satan, or his representative, that he intended to take Isaac to Mount Moriah and there sacrifice him to the Lord.

f. Satan, or his representative, did not *in the day that he heard it*, tell Abraham he was forbidden to sacrifice Isaac.

g. Abraham carried out God's instructions, believing as we are told in Hebrews, that God would restore Isaac to life.

h. God surprised everyone by accepting Isaac as a living sacrifice, accepting him as His slave.

i. Isaac had two sons, the elder of which God permitted to sell his birthright to the younger for a mess of pottage. The second-born son in this way acquired the rights of the firstborn and thus became (figuratively) God's firstborn.

Based on the above, we conclude

a. Jacob and all his family, including also his slaves, were God's slaves from a time long before the Exodus took place. God was dealing with His Own People throughout the 40 years of wandering in the desert and He has been throughout all history since.

b. Adam's foolish choice enslaved himself, Eve and all their descendants to Satan.

c. God, in putting the First Couple out of the Garden, was acting in love, not wrath as is so often preached and taught.

d. Because God freely chose not to disobey the laws He created for governing interactions between rational beings, He waited a very long time before acting to free His prized creation from slavery.

e. By giving Isaac to God as a living sacrifice, Abraham, still a slave to Satan, provided the seed for a race owing its allegiance to God.

f. That race, at the time of the Exodus and through history since was and remains God's property, His personal possession, His people, and the apple of His eye.

Step **6**. We found it unnecessary to amend the working hypothesis, axioms and assumptions because they led to an internally consistent understanding of the scriptures.

Step **7**. We now look at the New Testament to see if there is evidence of slaves of Satan living in Jesus' time, and if so, whether Jesus died to free them from slavery or to transfer ownership of Satan's slaves to God.

Our hypothesis suggests there must have been slaves living in Jesus' time, and Scripture confirms it. We have found ample supporting evidence and no contradictory evidence in the New Testament. Therefore we conclude:

There were slaves existing at the time of Jesus' self sacrifice.

As for the second question, there are several verses that attest to the fact that the redeemed were God's slaves, His property and no verses presenting an alternative. **We conclude: Jesus died not to set men free, but to transfer ownership from Satan to God.**

Step **8**: Our preliminary and final conclusions summarize the results of our investigation into the question of why Jesus died on the Cross. Publishing this paper satisfies the requirement to publish in an appropriate medium.

Preliminary Conclusions:

a. God's message sometimes is communicated by parables; this evidence supports our working hypothesis.

A Match Made In Heaven

b. God Created Adam a mortal man.

c. God created man to be free.

d. God warned Adam not to eat the forbidden fruit: – admonished him, not commanded him.

e. By choosing to listen to and act upon what the Serpent said instead of heeding God's warning, Adam – a free man – accepted Satan's lordship, and in so doing became his slave.

f. Adams' slavery was passed on to his children and their children, potentially forever.

g. A slave has no way of freeing himself. If he is to be free, his master must set him free

h. God's putting Adam and Eve out of the Garden was an act of love – not punishment. He was protecting them from eternal slavery.

i. The Flood Story teaches us that all humans are descendants of Adam.

j. The laws of Num 30:1 -16 apply not just to a man and his women, but also to a master and his slaves.

k. If a man or master does not forbid what his woman or slave has told him she or he intends to do, then the woman or slave is free to act as she or he intended to act.

l. Jacob and all his family, including also his slaves, were God's slaves from a time long before the Exodus took place. God was dealing with His Own People throughout the 40 years of wandering in the desert; He has been throughout all history since.

Final Conclusions:

    a. There were slaves of Satan living in Jesus' time.

    b. Jesus sacrificed himself not to set mankind free, but to transfer ownership of Satan's slaves to God the Father, so that He could justly permit them to choose to follow Him and gain eternal life.

    c. From the time of the Crucifixion onward, all men and women have from birth belonged to God; all now living are God's people.

    d. We have established a credible answer to the question, "Why Did Jesus Die on the Cross."

    e. **Step 9:** Preserve the records of all this. You will need them later to answer questions about your conclusions or your methods.

This hard copy plus backups on two hard drives satisfies this requirement.

www.ingramcontent.com/pod-product-compliance
Lightning Source LLC
Chambersburg PA
CBHW071456040426
42444CB00008B/1357